T0311554

Manager vs. Leader

Cutting through the clutter of management and leadership books, *Manager vs. Leader: Untying the Gordian Knot* works to differentiate the terms manager and leader. With these terms often used synonymously, misunderstanding leads to confusion and failed expectations at all levels of an organization. Providing both academic and practical organizational examples, this book challenges readers with ranging experience and knowledge to explore management and leadership in a new and comprehensive way.

Enabling readers to better understand the nuances between leading and managing, this book provides historical context while guiding readers in understanding the impact each role has within an organization. Through brief explorations into Organization Development and Transformation, this book works through the state of the leadership concept and provides insights into future challenges for managers and leaders.

Armed with historical context, a foundation to explore the terms manager and leader, and an open mind, readers will be able to more effectively manage expectations and interact with others whether professionally or personally.

Robert M. Murphy is a professor and lecturer in management, leadership and managing change. He is a retired US Army officer who has experience as commander, staff officer and as a researcher, and has lectured throughout Europe, Central America and China. He has academic experience as academic department chair and executive to university president for planning.

Kathleen M. Murphy is a professor and lecturer in management, entrepreneurship, negotiations and International Business. She has lectured throughout Europe, especially Poland. She was the university representative to Russia to study international education initiatives, and has taught management for a semester at Finance and Economics University, Yunnan, China.

Routledge Focus on Business and Management

For a complete list of titles in this series, please visit www.routledge.com/business/series/FBM

The fields of business and management have grown exponentially as areas of research and education. This growth presents challenges for readers trying to keep up with the latest important insights. Routledge Focus on Business and Management presents small books on big topics and how they intersect with the world of business.

Individually, each title in the series provides coverage of a key academic topic, whilst collectively, the series forms a comprehensive collection across the business disciplines.

ISSN: 2475–6369

Manager vs. Leader
Untying the Gordian Knot

**Robert M. Murphy and
Kathleen M. Murphy**

Routledge
Taylor & Francis Group

LONDON AND NEW YORK

First published 2018
by Routledge
2 Park Square, Milton Park, Abingdon, Oxon OX14 4RN

and by Routledge
605 Third Avenue, New York, NY 10017

First issued in paperback 2021

Routledge is an imprint of the Taylor & Francis Group, an informa business

British Library Cataloguing-in-Publication Data
A catalogue record for this book is available from the British Library

Library of Congress Cataloging-in-Publication Data
A catalog record for this book has been requested

ISBN 13: 978-1-03-209644-5 (pbk)
ISBN 13: 978-1-138-55908-0 (hbk)

Typeset in Times New Roman
by Apex CoVantage, LLC

This book is dedicated to the people who have taught us the most about organizational life . . . our children. We usually think about organizational life in terms of our work life but when we really sit down and think about it, family life is where we have learned our basic lessons about organizational life . . . both the good and the bad lessons.

So we dedicate this book to our first teachers:

Christopher

Kelli

Kathleen, Jr.

Kerri

Erinrose

Thank you for your support and patience.

Contents

Figures

Preface

The purpose for this book is to help readers better understand the nuances between being a leader and being a manager. This text should help guide and apprise the reader of the impact these roles play on decision-making efforts as organizations evolve, especially during transformative times.

The journey of this book began over forty years ago when Robert was teaching leadership and management to young college students. What he read in the various texts did not match up to what he was observing in real life as a young US Army officer. Throughout his years of teaching, further education, and interface with business, educational, and military leaders, it became obvious that the confusion between the concepts of management and leadership was widespread in organizational life and misunderstood by the general public. What was also prevalent was the resistance by each sector of society to agree on terminology and definitions for these terms. Robert conducted simple exercises in his lectures that confirmed what he was observing and proved that confusion did exist between the terms 'leader' and 'manager.' Although not a rigorous sampling test, these simple exercises reinforced his theory and inspired the authors to dig deeper into qualifying the nuances and differences between the terms 'leader' and 'manager.'

The authors are aware that the book world is filled with college textbooks and 'how to' books on techniques to become better managers and leaders. However, the terms 'leader' and 'manager' are used synonymously without a thorough understanding of each. This misunderstanding causes failed expectations at all levels of organizations.

This book is unique because it starts with the premise that many people do not really understand these concepts, and although this reality might not sit well with many sectors of our society, it is crucial to lay a foundation and explore these terms in order to more successfully and effectively interact with others, whether in our professional or personal lives.

This book lays a foundation for the history and basic concepts of management and leadership that are taught in today's universities. The book is not designed to be a replacement for a regular college course in management but rather to lay a firm foundation for all readers. This foundation is crucial in order to understand the dynamics as to why so many people seem to be frustrated with their purported leaders in their respective organizations, be it a small local business, an international corporation, or even an elected government official. The distinction between the two terms also becomes important for people in today's organizations. Through reading this book and exploring the nuances of the terms 'manager' and 'leader,' people can more realistically adjust their expectations of their managers and leaders as they face the challenges in the ever-changing landscape of our society.

Finally, because organizational life affects all our lives, this book was written with the hope that it would appeal to people in general regardless of the type of organization they are associated with. While Robert was teaching at the United States Army War College, businesspeople would come in to consult with faculty to find out why the military is so successful as a cohesive organization. It was relayed to them that besides building a sound corporate culture, it is important that each member receive professional development at various stages of their careers. This is especially true for those individuals who move from frontline supervisory roles, through middle management, to the executive level of their organization. This unfortunately is not true in other types of organizations. While Robert and Kathy taught MBA courses, students would explain that they were getting an MBA just to check the block in their resume. When they go back to their organizations, the new knowledge they gained is overshadowed by traditional ways of doing business or by organizational politics. The hope is that with the material presented in this book, people will not return to the traditional ways in their organization that are creating dysfunctionality, but rather find better ways to work toward organizational goals.

Acknowledgments

There have been many relatives, friends, colleagues, and students who have been instrumental in our journey writing this book. It would take another book to thank them all. Yet we must single out one person who has been absolutely critical in producing our final manuscript. She just happens to be our oldest grandchild who has turned into a fine, intelligent woman whom we both are very proud of.

While in the midst of our writing efforts, we realized that although both of us have published many articles and a few books, we needed a good professional editor to keep us in tow. After a while, we realized that we already had such a person in our own family, namely, our granddaughter Aislinn Murphy. She already had a bachelor's degree in English and had just completed a master's degree in Public Relations.

So we want to thank all those who helped us along our journey, but we send a special thanks to Aislinn Murphy for taking us the rest of the way.

Introduction

Overview

In this day and age, the terms 'leader' and 'manager' seem to be synonymous. After all, they are literally tied together, right? Wrong! Subtleties exist between the two terms and it is important to recognize each term and its core meaning. It is only then that individuals can develop more realistic expectations of those identified as either a manager or a leader.

An often-heard criticism when distinguishing between these two terms is that the two words are interchangeable and any attempt to differentiate is 'semantics.' However, in defining what words mean, individuals in organizations have a greater chance of adapting and managing change by more clearly comprehending and defining everyone's role within the group.

In conversations with managers and leaders in the workplace and executive-level students, many mention that even though they have had good experiences, perhaps their experiences could have been more fruitful with a deeper understanding of the dynamics of these two concepts. Others who have had some bad experiences have neutral feelings or worse in that they view management as a necessary evil. The reality is that management lies somewhere between a necessary process and the mechanism that often restricts critical thinking and creativity.

Today we live in a world of real-time access to events happening around the world. The information we receive from news programs, the Internet, and other sources is a factor in how each individual perceives reality. In organizations, we depend on managers and leaders to help sort through this flow of information and validate what is accurate and what is not. Realistically, more weight is put on those called leaders to get it right. Unfortunately, there exists conflicting information and it is often difficult to objectively ascertain what information and which sources are valid and reliable. Using this example, the underlying hypothesis for this book is that this condition of sorting out reality as to who is a manager and who is a leader is a real problem in organizations today. More importantly, because of this dilemma, the misunderstanding between manager and leader leads to false expectations of what is required from each. Exploring and defining each term can guide readers in their expectations of managers and leaders.

Is this dilemma real?

In a review of some current college textbooks (Robbins and Coulter, 2013; Schermerhorn, 1996) and a classic book on management (Drucker, 1994), we found more of a consensus on the definition of management than for leadership. The clarity around the term 'manager' seems in large part attributable to the fact that managers are in a position to make administrative decisions and are part of the organization's hierarchy. On the other hand, a 'leader' is a term used to describe how an individual's actions influence others to rethink their personal value system. Unfortunately, society uses the word 'leader' to describe so many different types of people, causing the word to become one of the most overused, misunderstood, and convoluted concepts in corporate, government, military, and religious organizations. We often hear the word 'leader' used to describe a top performer on a sports team, the first person to present an idea on any subject, or an executive in an organization be it a business, government, or religious official. In interfacing with people in education, business, military, government, and religious organizations, some may find that these individuals often talk past one another and that each sector of society has developed its own vocabulary to address its organizational situation.

To validate this confusion over the concepts of manager and leader, informal experiments were conducted by the authors to determine if these concepts have reached a point where they have lost their value to portray a specific meaning. The first experiment was conducted in 2000 when Robert presented a paper at an international conference in Budapest, Hungary. The audience for this presentation included both academic and business individuals. The paper being presented was titled "Strategic Management vs. Strategic Leadership: Untying the Gordian Knot," which is the foundation for this book. The methodology included presenting ten definitions from numerous college textbooks, with five of the definitions describing management while the other five described leadership, shown in Figures 0.2 and 0.3. The audience was then challenged to differentiate between the definitions for management and those for leadership. No one got more than

50 percent right and worse yet, some argued that a specific definition was not that of leadership as had been listed but rather was the definition of management. The point here is that if a consensus cannot be established from businesspeople and educators, how can we expect people who are not subject matter experts to understand these operating concepts?

To test yourself, examine the slides that were used at the presentation in Budapest (Figure 0.1). See if you can choose which definitions are for leadership and which are for management. Take a piece of paper and next to the number write "leadership" or "management."

It is not as easy as you thought it might be, is it? After the presentation, Robert felt the embarrassment and frustration of his audience that you may now be experiencing. The attendees most likely had a new respect for the frustration that students and workers feel as they try to understand these concepts. It goes a long way to understand why most people go to the default position of equating the two concepts.

To give you a better sense of the magnitude of the frustration, the next two slides give you what the authors of the college texts identify as the definitions for leading and managing.

---

1. The set of processes used to get members of the organization to work together to advance the interest of the organization (Griffin, 1999, p. 10).
2. The process of arousing enthusiasm and directing human-resource efforts toward organizational directives (Schermerhorn, 1996, p. G5).
3. The process of directing and supporting others in pursuit of the organization's mission and goals (Hess & Siciliano, 1996, p. 256).
4. The function of managers involving influencing people so that they will contribute to organization and group goals; it has to do predominantly with the interpersonal aspect of management (Weihrich & Koontz, 1993, p. 256).
5. A set of activities directed at an organization's resources (human, financial, physical, and information) with the aim of achieving organizational goals in an efficient and effective manner (Griffin, 1999, p. 5).
6. The coordination of human, material, technological, and financial resources needed for an organization to achieve its goals (Hess & Siciliano, 1996, p. 6).
7. The process of getting things done through the efforts of others (Mondy & Premeaux, 1994, p. 5).
8. The process of designing & maintaining an environment in which individuals work together in groups to accomplish efficiently selected aims (Weihrich & Koontz, 1993, p. 4).

Figure 0.1 Managing and leading definitions

Leadership

1. The set of processes used to get members of the organization to work together to advance the interest of the organization (Griffin, 1999, p. 10).

2. The process of arousing enthusiasm and directing human-resource efforts toward organizational directives (Schermerhorn, 1996, p. G5).

3. The process of directing and supporting others in pursuit of the organization's mission and goals (Hess & Siciliano, 1996, p. 256).

4. The function of managers involving influencing people so that they will contribute to organization and group goals; it has to do predominantly with the interpersonal aspect of management (Weihrlich & Koontz, 1993, p. 490).

Figure 0.2 Managing and leading definitions (leadership)

Management

5. A set of activities directed at an organization's resources (human, financial, physical, and information) with the aim of achieving organizational goals in an efficient and effective manner (Griffin, 1999, p. 5).

6. The coordination of human, material, technological, and financial resources needed for an organization to achieve its goals (Hess & Siciliano, 1996. p. 6).

7. The process of getting things done through the efforts of others (Mondy & Premeaux, 1994, p. 6).

8. The process of designing & maintaining an environment in which individuals work together in groups to accomplish efficiently selected aims (Weihrich & Koontz, 1993, p. 4).

Figure 0.3 Managing and leading definitions (management)

Why the Gordian Knot?

The imagery of the Gordian Knot in the subtitle of the book is used to project the complexity of defining the terms 'leaders' and 'managers.' The term 'Gordian Knot' is used to identify an exceedingly complicated problem that can only be solved by a bold act. The term dates back to Alexander the Great's time in the middle of the fourth century. As this ancient story unfolds, King Gordius used an intricate knot to lash a chariot to a pole, which purportedly could only be untied by the future conqueror of Asia. Alexander the Great, after struggling to untie the knot through traditional

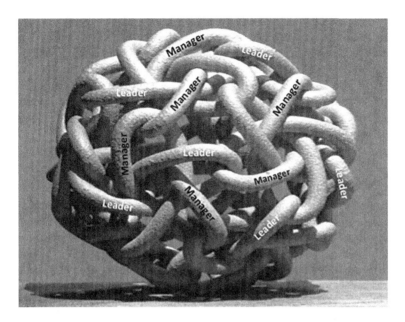

Figure 0.4 The Gordian Knot

means, finally resorted to using his sword to cut his way through the knot. Thus today, the phrase "cutting the Gordian Knot" has come to mean a bold solution to a complicated problem. Let's hope that the authors' sword is sharp enough to provide a bold solution to differentiate and justify the importance of the distinction between the terms 'manager' and 'leader.'

The path of the book

Now that the symbolism of the Gordian Knot and how it applies to explaining leadership versus management has been addressed, the purpose of this literary effort is to cut through this knot of management versus leadership to lay a firm foundation on the differences between the two concepts. As explained above, the authors feel strongly that this book applies to all of us who live in organizations. And, that really means all of us.

This foundation will enable those individuals who have never taken a formal course in management to enhance their understanding of these two organizational concepts that permeate all types of institutions, including families, businesses, the military, academia, government agencies, and even religious units. To do this, a brief history of management also will be explored in order to show the robustness of this concept and to fix its generally accepted parameters. As for the field of leadership, the general concepts will be laid out but as mentioned above, there exists so many views as to what leadership is that it is sometimes hard to get one's arms around the concept. The plan is to dissect this concept into present-day usages and then address perceived weaknesses of these usages. By now you probably have surmised that the authors strongly believe that there is a real difference between managers and leaders. Let us hope that the case made in this book is strong enough that you will agree.

A final note

The first five chapters present the traditional approach at understanding the concepts of management and leadership; however, in Chapter 6 we will address the challenges that managers and leaders may face in the future. With the evolution of organizations to structures that range from traditional Mechanistic structures to Chaordic, a blending of chaos and order, structures and including the infinite variations in between, it becomes imperative to define and describe responsibilities of managers and leaders as best as we can. This allows people at all levels of an organization to adjust their expectations. Will this result in a perfect alignment between the worlds of managers and leaders? No, but it will mitigate the looseness that exists in these terms and in the end, provide a better chance to lessen the turbulence in the evolution of organizations.

Chapter 7, "Conclusions," presents our gold nuggets that derive from years of interfacing with managers, leaders, students and academic colleagues. We realize that some people will question our insights, but we feel that they will incite excellent group discussions regardless of the type of organization.

1 The evolution of management thought

Overview

This chapter establishes a foundation allowing for the opportunity to fully explore the differences between these two concepts. Although this book is not designed to replace a college textbook on management and leadership, this chapter presents a common foundation where readers of varied backgrounds can follow the analysis.

A brief history of management

The practice of management has been with us throughout recorded time. Egyptians in building the pyramids, Romans in performing their extraordinary engineering feats, and the myriad of other civilizations that have come and gone have all used some form of management to build and maintain their empires. However, management did not receive serious attention until the late 1800s. The attention was the result of the exponential growth of the factory system during this period, that is, the beginning of the Industrial Revolution. Wren (1972) credited Phyllis Deane (1965) for pinpointing the differences between pre-industrialized and industrialized nations using such factors as per capita income, economic growth, dependence on agriculture, degree of specialization labor, and geographical integration of markets. "Using these factors as indicators, Deane concluded that the shift in England from pre-industrial to an industrial nation became most evident in 1750 and accelerated thereafter" (Wren, 1972, p. 37).

Since World War II, the study and practice of management underwent some revolutionary changes in its theoretical constructs, techniques, methods, and tools. Today with the work on complexity theory, and the crossovers from the New Sciences to the field of management espoused by Margaret Wheatley (1999), the robustness of the field of management is growing to a point where it becomes imperative that managers and leaders stay abreast of

Figure 1.1 Evolution of management thought

the balance between the well-grounded concepts of the past and the seemingly daily revelations of new techniques in management.

To lay out the evolution of management in an understandable sequence, Figure 1.1 shows Bateman and Zeithaml's (1993) timeline of some of the major categories of management thought since the early 1900s. Although management thought has evolved over time, valuable insight can still be gained from older schools of thought.

To help better understand the categories in Figure 1.1, here is a brief explanation of these categories:

Systematic Management: The organization, supervision and oversight of the conduct of business activity based on rational processes and procedures; a formalization of a holistic view of work activity.

Scientific Management: The management of a business, industry, or economy, according to principles of efficiency derived from experiments in methods of work and production, especially from time-and-motion studies; the effort to bring the Scientific method to the workplace.

Bureaucracy: A rational and efficient form of an organization founded on logic, order and legitimate authority. See Chapter 2 for more details.

Administrative Management: The theory generally calls for a formalized administrative structure, a clear division of labor, and delegation of power and authority to administrators relevant to their areas of responsibilities. This approach to management stresses the design structure in order to continue with Weber's work on the concept of bureaucratic organization.

Organizational Behavior: The study of individuals and their behavior within the context of the organization in a workplace setting. This branch of management started to humanize the workforce in lieu of treating workers as if they were machines.

Systems Theory: An approach to industrial relations that likens the enterprise to an organism with interdependent parts, each with its own specific function and interrelated responsibilities.

Contingency Theory: A theory that claims that there is no best way to organize a corporation, to lead a company, or to make decisions. Instead, the optimal course of action is contingent (dependent) upon the internal and external situation.

New Sciences Management Theory: An integration of how new discoveries in quantum physics, chaos theory, and biology challenge our standard ways of thinking in and about organizations.

Although many people tend to disavow the classical management literature, much of our current understanding of people at work is a result of the pioneering work of classical management thinkers. Frederick Taylor, Henri Fayol, the Gilbreths, Mary Parker Follett, Henry Gantt, and Max Weber are classical management thinkers who helped move the concept of management from an agriculture society driven by lords and masters in charge of peasants to one of a more rational and scientific approach. This evolution of how society constructed itself was primarily due to the challenges of the Industrial Revolution that compelled organizations to better use and focus their resources.

Sadly many of today's managers and leaders take these new concepts and try to apply them without a full understanding of the other factors that are usually at play in solving organizational problems. To overcome this shortfall, Chapter 2 is presented to provide the historical anchors to management concepts that are still viable today. The challenge is to take these concepts and build the bridges needed to recognize their applications in the various activities in today's organization. The message here is to be wary of any quick fixes that do not fully account for past solutions to organizational problems. This is especially true when examining why past solutions were changed or why they should be continued. The key always has been and always will be the use of critical thinking by managers, leaders, and others at every level of the organization. Only then can they sort through the myriad of factors that affect organizational problems and weigh solutions accordingly.

What is Critical Thinking? According to Jane Willsen (1996), "Critical thinking is a systematic way to form and shape one's thinking" (p. 419). "It is . . . disciplined, comprehensive, based on intellectual standards, and as a result well-reasoned" (p. 1996). In other words, this is the formal process that is used to determine the truth and validity of consumed materials in people's lives. However, everyone does not possess the knowledge base or skill set to fully implement this process, which invariably leads to the differences we have as human beings. Some may challenge the definition above, but after operational definitions have been sorted out, most will probably agree that some phenomenon is being referenced despite the term used.

The foundation for critical thinking is the scientific method, which is defined as the process of investigating phenomena, acquiring new knowledge, and correcting or integrating previous knowledge. To be termed 'scientific,' a method of inquiry must be based on empirical and measurable evidence subject to specific principles of reasoning for analyzing observations or questions about events. Too often the problem with the application of this process seems to be the resistance in applying scientific methodology. Without going into the quagmire of why people resist the use of science and math, especially during their school years, the use of valid, reliable data in their decision-making process is crucial in critical thinking. Especially in today's world where we are flooded by all sorts of information and too often marketing experts, salespeople or politicians use our lack of effort to seek valid, reliable evidence against us.

To add to this problem, most people do not seek knowledge outside of their specialty areas hindering their ability to independently investigate events, concepts, and facts from many perspectives before information is placed in the knowledge base and deemed valid and reliable.

The Third Wave

In Alvin Toffler's *The Third Wave* (1980), which is the second book in his trilogy on the changing face of civilization, he uses a model to set the tone for a global view of human evolution in organizational settings. In the Third Wave, Toffler points out that if you step back and look at the major movements of civilized society, there seems to be three major categories or waves of societal evolution, see Figure 1.2.

As humans moved from the Hunter-Gatherer stage of existence into a more stable life style where people cultivated the land, the change caused societal pressure on how humanity organized itself. This first wave Toffler called the Agriculture Wave. In this stage, the organizational emphasis revolved around a farming existence. As a result, the need for large pools of labor gave rise to the feudal system, slavery, and the need for large families. The management style was a dictatorial system that emphasized tight control measures. Some of the other organizational characteristics of this life style were little to no formal education for the masses and work routines based on seasonal changes. These characteristics of how man organized himself for work would later present themselves as problematic as society moved into the Second Wave, Industrialization.

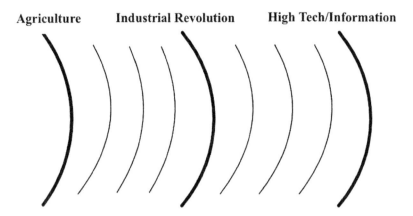

Agriculture   **Industrial Revolution**   **High Tech/Information**

Figure 1.2 Toffler's Third Wave analogy

The Second Wave has been, and continues to be, a shock to the freedom of man in the workplace. To deal with this shock, a body of knowledge concerning factory, job design, and personnel issues had to be addressed in this evolving work environment. In a short period of time, workers' skills were transformed from handicraft skills to machine operation skills. Additionally, to control the large volume of uneducated workers, increased levels of management were established. In addition to these increased levels of management, the use of Standard Operating Procedures (SOPs) was needed to focus and synchronize the workforce effort. In reality, in-depth planning processes were needed at all levels of these industrialized complexes in order to keep abreast of the exploding landscape of the Second Wave.

As an aside, many of us today are products of the socialization that evolved from the Second Wave developments. Our vocabulary, our educational process, our governmental systems, the structures of our buildings, and the way we think about civilization are all products of a Second Wave mentality. Problems that this mindset creates will become clear as the Third Wave is explored.

While this new industrialized organization afforded higher levels of efficiency and greater production, it also uncovered a critical problem, namely, mutual dependence. Since the production line was normally a piecemeal operation where workers were tied to a conveyor system, workers were now required to be at a designated station at a specific time. This work configuration was far different from the farm and craftsman routines that people were accustomed to; i.e., flexible routines where workers were, for the most part, free to set their own schedules. Now, start, break, and quit times are all regulated. Following regimented plans and SOPs became stifling to the workers. This would change with the rise of the Third Wave where maximum flexibility and less rigidity of rules and policies seem to be the new mode of operation. Notice that there was not an absence of rules and policies but rather some built-in flexibility due to the increased education, acquired experiences of the workforce, and the fluidity of the marketplace.

The last Toffler Wave is the most troubling. If moving human society from the caves to the farms to the manufacturing plant floor was not tough enough, he now foretells that humanity is challenged with an ever-increasing crescendo of new industries that would take center stage. This center stage is one where organizational complexity and chaos is the norm and the rate of change is exponential. As a result, the changes for this wave are so overwhelming that the task for organizational decision makers to find historical trends to base timely decisions on is increasingly elusive. Toffler points out that industries involving computers, electronics, information, biotechnology, and the financial industry would begin to influence the direction of the world's economy. He continued by saying some of the features of these industries would be flexible manufacturing, niche markets, the spread of part-time work, and the demassification of the media. This Third Wave continues today, nearly twenty-four years after Toffler identified this phenomenon.

A key takeaway from Toffler's Third Wave model is that the world is living through all three waves at the same time. Consequently, it brings into focus an understanding of the structural friction that these waves cause in organizations. In fact, it is safe to say that a key factor for the turmoil in many countries today is due to the societal friction caused by addressing all three waves at the same time, either within their own country or in other countries existing in different Toffler Waves attempting to work together.

Addressing change in organizations be it in a family, educational institution, workplace or a country is a daunting task because there are obstacles to change within the organization as well as external forces pressuring the organization to evolve to a more viable existence. The use of the Kurt Lewin Change model is helpful to better grasp this idea. In Figure 1.3, an adaptation of Lewin's model by Cummings and Huse (1989, p. 99) assists in a better understanding of the process. This figure shows just some of the factors that are pushing organizations to more desirable levels of performance while other factors present obstacles for improvement. While this diagram is an oversimplification, it represents an overall understanding of some of the forces at play.

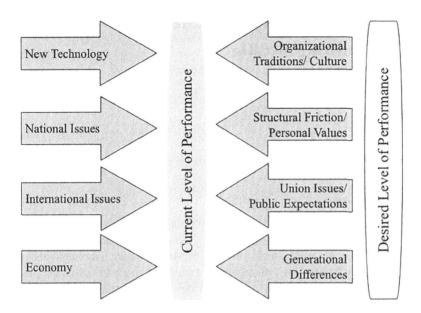

Figure 1.3 Forces influencing change

With Toffler's Wave model now in our analytical skills' toolkit, the task at hand is to gain an understanding of the various management concepts that have been put forth throughout the years. These concepts by themselves are not a final solution for any organizational dilemma, but the concepts certainly can give important insights to a manager or leader trying to take their organizations through the challenges they face both today and in the future.

2 Classical approaches to management

Overview

This chapter highlights the historical contributions made to the discipline of Management. Our experiences with executives, workers and students reveal that most people have a narrower view of Management. This continues to build a foundation of how management started and how it has evolved. This is important because it allows us to show how the management process was formulated and why it is evolving over time. This foundation is especially important because it sets the stage for transformational change and why knowing the distinctions between a manager or a leader is critical.

Scientific management

Frederick W. Taylor is generally considered the 'Father of Scientific Management.' Although he was from a family of means, Taylor worked his way up from a metal apprentice through the common labor ranks to become the 'gang boss' at Midvale Steel. Eventually, promotions through the ranks led him to become the chief engineer while still a young man. Recognizing his lack of scientific education, he eventually received a mechanical engineering degree through a home study course. Armed with his years of experience as a common laborer and his newly obtained formal education, Taylor proceeded to search for a "science of work" (Wren, 1972, pp. 111–116).

Taylor (1911) in his book, *The Principles of Scientific Management*, summarizes what he perceived to be the domains of management (cited in Schermerhorn, 1996, pp. 28–29). They are:

- a science of managing, complete with rules and principles in lieu of rule-of-thumb methods
- a system to scientifically select, train and develop workers to replace the traditional method where workers chose their own work and trained themselves

- an effort to institute a cooperative effort with workers to ensure that all work was performed in accordance with principles of science that were developed for the work being performed
- an effort to establish an equal division of the work and responsibilities between workers and management for which they are better fitted to perform.

The United States Army applied Taylor's principles when Major General William Crozier, the Army's Chief of Ordnance for sixteen years, applied the methods of Scientific Management in Army arsenals in the early 1900s. The use of Scientific Management philosophies was instrumental in preparing the arsenals for the burden that would be placed on them during World War I. Before thinking that the tenets of Scientific Management are no longer applicable, one needs to only look at today's practices to see that these have become an integral part of our organizations. Job descriptions, incentive plans, hiring practices, career management, and training programs are but a few of today's programs that have their beginnings in the Scientific Management movement.

As Taylor and his colleagues were preaching the tenets of Scientific Management in America, Max Weber, a German intellectual, became a leading thinker in understanding the relationships between nineteenth-century male-dominated family-firms, which he called "patrimonial," and the emerging era of large-scale organizations of industry and government in Europe (Wren, 1972, p. 229).

The birth of bureaucracies

It is unfortunate that Weber has been tarred with the bureaucracy label that, in today's society, is blamed for the many downfalls of organizations. When taken into a historical perspective, Weber's real contribution to the field of management was his zest for intellectual analysis of organizations. Today we call it critical thinking.

Max Weber's writings, lectures, and thinking in general provided a model to search for more efficient and effective ways to organize people at work. The main dilemma for Weber was to bridge the conceptual underpinnings of the two prevalent ideologies of his time, namely "The Protestant Work Ethic" and "Capitalism." In Wren's book (1972, pp. 231–232) on the evolution of management thought, he credits Weber's research, which led him to form what he considered to be the characteristics of an "Ideal Bureaucracy," namely:

- rules and procedures
- clear division of labor

- hierarchy of authority
- advancement based on technical competence
- separation of ownership from management of organizations
- rights and property belong to the organization
- documentation of all decisions, rules, and actions.

The tenets of Weber, outlined above, are familiar to individuals working within large organizations today. Most would say that the tenets have been applied to the detriment of the workplace as they bemoan the use of rules and procedures stifling their daily work lives. The response to these concerns is that employees too often internalize these rules and procedures to the point of following them blindly without understanding how it affects customers and the overarching goals of the organization.

To illustrate the need for the use of these organizational measures, in lectures by the authors the concept of Autokinesis is presented in Figure 2.1. The question posed with this figure is "What happens to a light in a totally dark room?" It is noted that the light is not bright enough to illuminate the room.

After some wild guesses by the audience, they are told that the light is bouncing around. The reason for this they are told is that the observation of motion is always relative to a reference point. In darkness or in a featureless environment, there is no reference point to fix the position of objects; consequently, the movement of a single point is undefined.

The teaching point in this analogy references what Weber was advocating; namely, there needs to be organizational mechanisms like Standard

Figure 2.1 Autokinesis

Operating Procedures (SOPs), rules, and plans in place to focus the efforts of people in the organization. Of course, the problem is always a balancing act between the fixed directives of the organization and the innovative and creative acts of the workers. Too many rules tend to restrict a worker's initiative, innovation, and creativity while too few guidelines cause workers to perform in ways that may be problematic for the organization as a whole. This occurs in organizations when subunits of an organization fight for resources during the budgeting process. March and Simon in their classic book, *Organizations*, addressed the struggles companies have in establishing a healthy collective effort to reach company goals (Wren, 1972, p. 466). Today we have a name for this issue. It is called "suboptimization" and is used to explain the tension between making decisions to optimize subordination units in an organization at the expense of the effectiveness and efficiency of the whole organization. This cartoon shown in Figure 2.2 makes this point. The main bar representatives the path to accomplish the organization's mission and goals while the snakes below represent the proverbial snake pit where subunits fight for their groups' interests (rice bowls). The point is that optimization of subunits can cause suboptimization of the organization.

Although many readers will have stories of their own from organizations they are or have been in, a classic illustration of this phenomenon in action today is the United States congressional system. Article I of the United States Constitution establishes a Senate and the House of Representatives

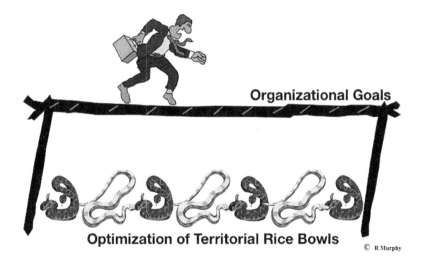

Figure 2.2 Suboptimization

with the powers, responsibilities, and criteria for selection of its members. In reality, what is happening is the institutionalization of suboptimization. That is, senators and representatives are elected from different communities throughout the country to represent their constituents' interest in the policies that are enacted. Although it is recognized that senators and representatives are integral to the collective national effort to help govern the country, it creates a struggle for these senators and representatives to balance the needs of their respective constituencies with the optimization of the whole, namely, doing what is best for the country. The pros and cons of this phenomenon is beyond the scope of this text, but it is noteworthy to demonstrate that structuring any organization can face built-in struggles during the planning phase regardless how thoughtful the effort. The bottom line is that suboptimization thresholds need to be pointed out in the planning phase and considered as the plan is being executed.

Although there appears to have been an overuse of a strict bureaucratic system in many organizations today, there remains a need for structures that have the characteristics listed above. What people seem to dislike about bureaucracies is the internalization of the rules to the point where employees dehumanize customers and fellow workers when communicating with them. The challenge for people in organizations is to continue to use rules and procedures to guide and focus their energies while rethinking Weber's characteristics in the context of today's new operating environment. As an example, Peter Drucker, the father of Modern Management Theory, pointed out that managers are akin to symphony conductors. In this scenario, the individual talents of their workers needed to be blended in such a way as to optimize the achievement of organizational goals. Too much input from one section or not enough from another alters the effectiveness and efficiency of the entire work effort. This balance is key.

During Max Weber's time, the workplace was rampant with nepotism and an environment that lent itself to the whims of its owners. Weber's efforts were designed to formalize the operations of the workplace as well as to help institutionalize the 'management class.' With the rise of these managers within publicly owned companies, a body of knowledge was needed to guide this new class of managers. It should be noted that the decision-making authority of these top managers was not absolute. In addition to the invisible hand of the marketplace to determine the viability of a manager's decision, an organizational mechanism also was established to protect the interest of the shareholders. This mechanism became the Board of Directors. This board not only has the ultimate authority for key decisions on such matters as policies, fiscal matters, and key personnel hirings but also the collective responsibility for the performance of the organization which, in many cases, is legally binding.

The search for an administrative process

A French mining engineer, Henri Fayol, provided one of the most significant contributions to the field of management during the Classical Management period. Like Taylor in America, Fayol gained extensive experience while working in an industry reeling from the effects of the birth of the Industrial Revolution. In 1888, he became the managing director of an iron foundry company that had severe financial difficulties. Faced with bankruptcy, Fayol used his own experiences to develop an "administrative process" that would delineate those factors that guided the success of organizations that he studied in Europe (Wren, 1972, p. 218).

In several of his writings, Fayol, as referenced in Wren, laid out his now-famous fourteen principles. They are:

1 Division of Work
2 Authority
3 Discipline
4 Unity of Command
5 Unity of Direction
6 Subordination of interest to the general interest
7 Remuneration
8 Centralization
9 Scalar Chain
10 Order
11 Equity
12 Stability of tenure of personnel
13 Initiative
14 Esprit de corps

Fayol's unique contribution to the field of management was that he recognized and codified a process by which all organizations should be governed. Following the work of Henri Fayol, management writers, practitioners, and academics have reworked his fourteen principles into four or five categories that are taught in most business schools today. Although some of the categories may be shaded one way or another, there is general agreement on the 'Management Process.' Additionally, it is also recognized that even though there has been debate on the distinction between governing, managing, administering, and commanding, it is generally accepted that this management process is universal to all types of organizations.

This is a critical point that will help us later in the book as the differences between management and leadership are distinguished. Over the years of working with both managers and leaders, the authors have discovered that many of the differences are due to operational definitions and not conceptual underpinnings. Too often people talk by one another because they are using different definitions that are based on their individual disciplines and career fields. Happily, once people take time to define what they mean by a specific concept, observation, or variable, it usually results in a unified common ground.

To this end, Figure 2.3 is a schematic that depicts this universal process with the respective meanings of the functions that evolved from Fayol's fourteen general principles. The functions depicted in Figure 2.3 capture the essence of Fayol's message to us, namely, that all organizations, regardless of mission or culture, are integral to one another in the management process; i.e., a process designed to focus the energy of an organization in order to accomplish a common purpose.

To emphasize this point, in 1975 while teaching a management class, Robert formed a panel consisting of the publisher from the local newspaper, a hospital administrator, the Provost of the university, and the senior military officer from the ROTC department. The members of the panel were then assigned a separate function of the management process and asked to discuss how they applied the function in their organization. It soon became obvious to the students that the concept of management was not a business

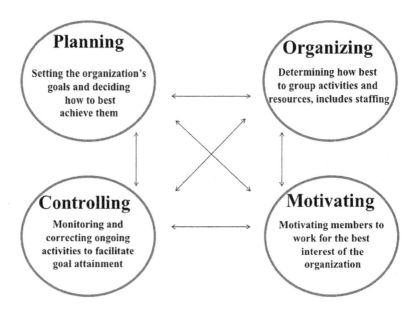

Figure 2.3 Management process (POMC model)

phenomenon, but rather an organizational one. In essence, the concept of management involves systems thinking at each level of any organization (Murphy, 1975).

Listening to people today talk about management, what appears to be missing is an understanding as to the robustness of this discipline. Too often when administrators, managers, and leaders start managing change within their organizations, little regard is given to the systemic effects that occur to the other functions of the management process. In effect, what happens is that as changes are made to the organization, the result is mixed messages to workers between old systems that are not revalidated and the newly instituted systems. To help flesh out this reality, Figure 2.3 provides a description for each function. In Griffin's text (2013), he uses leading where we prefer the term 'motivating.' The reason for the change is the basis for our book; namely, we see a deeper distinction between leading and management that needs to be explored. Griffin's illustration, however, helps to provide a deeper operational understanding to address the theoretical underpinning of such fields of change management as Strategic Management, Organization Development, and Organizational Transformation. Additionally, it also allows a more fundamental separation of the concepts of leader and manager.

The POMC model

Planning

Within the concept of planning, there are four general levels. For each level, there is an approximate time frame in which this planning occurs. Figure 2.4 provides a baseline to understand the various levels of planning. Be advised, these are only general categories. Each type of organization needs to articulate through operational definitions the specific time frames and labels that are applicable to its industry. There is general agreement that in regard to planning, there exists a hierarchy in which levels of plans must be tightly coordinated to ensure that the energy of the organization is focused and optimized.

Many parts of the world community are presently in the High Tech/Information Age. As a result, the time frames depicted are rapidly collapsing into shorter time periods. Traditionally, strategic planning involved visioning beyond the five-year horizon. Today, companies in the computer industry think of strategic planning in terms of less than five years. Although time frames are getting shorter, there still remains the necessity to have planning phases in order to allow a systematic, timely flow of activities from a draft board vision to the execution of the desired product or service to the customer.

* **Strategic (planning horizon)**
* **Long Term (5+ years)**
* **Middle Term (1-5 years)**
* **Short Term (~1 year)**

The planning horizon time frame is dependent on the type of industry, reliability and validity of forecast indicators, and how much risk the organization is willing to endure.

Figure 2.4   The planning function

The word 'strategic' unfortunately seems to be a confusing word especially when it is used in relation to tactical plans based on strategies as well as the long-term path of the organization determined through the Strategic Planning process. Thus, as shown in Figure 2.4, the first type of planning occurs at the strategic level where a long-term comprehensive analysis is conducted to achieve the vision and mission of an organization. This effort includes planning at each level of an organization in order to achieve a coordinated endeavor. You also hear the term 'strategies.' Strategies, when used in this sense, refer to how the organization will accomplish its mission and long-term goals. Figure 2.5 lays this out through the use of an American football analogy.

Another illustration is based on a phrase often heard as a great example of a vision statement, namely, President John F. Kennedy's vision to put a man on the moon. There is no argument that it inspired the United States to match the former USSR in a race to outer space. However, the race to the moon was just one goal to engage the United States in outer space activities. A more inclusive way of phrasing this challenge is shown in Figure 2.6. Although the example does not expand the full text that NASA probably articulated in its Strategic Planning process, it does give the scope that its inclusive vision should capture the complexity of entering space.

This example is offered because too many vision and mission statements are merely public relations statements from the company. In fact, in talking with some people in these organizations, two issues arose. First, the strategic plan is a required document to have but does not leave the shelf. Second, too many of the activities and decisions are made in the organization that do not flow from the strategic plan. Simply put, there should be no actions occurring in an

Vision: **Be the best football team ever**

Mission: **Win Super bowl(s)/Games**

Goal: **Score Touchdowns**

Objectives: **Get 1st downs – 10 yards; defensive stops**

Strategies: **Running & throwing attacks; defense schemes**

Figure 2.5 Planning terminology

Vision: To become the leading country in space technology

Mission: To become the world leader in space exploration, satellite communication, and SETI*

Goals: 1. Space Exploration: Americans on the moon by the end of the decade; explore Mars and solar system

2. Satellite Communication: Establish a GPS**; establish a telecommunication system

3. SETI: Establish an agency to establish a program

* SETI: Search for Extraterrestrial Intelligence
** GPS: Global Positioning System

Figure 2.6 Another example of planning terminology

organization that do not flow from the strategic plan, or more specifically, the mission statement. Strategic managers, and especially strategic leaders, may want to push the boundaries of the vision and mission statement in order to secure the continued viability of their organization, but the strategic plan and subsequent plans need to be changed in order to reflect this new direction. The caveat, of course, is that this direction must be done in such a way as to be in sync with the present-day capabilities. As always, the key is to find a balance between current resources and the vision for the future. This will become an important point when we discuss the evolution of the POMC model.

As important as Strategic Planning is, caution must be instilled in the process. Henry Mintzberg, in his book *The Rise and Fall of Strategic Planning* (1994), presented a critical caution regarding Strategic Planning. Mintzberg, who was the former president of the Strategic Management Society, chastised himself and others for their blind allegiance to the Strategic Planning process. His contentions rest with the search for the definitive, quantifiable solution for the future. He shows how planning can stifle commitment, narrow an organization's vision, make change impossible, and cater to the politics of an organization. Mintzberg's position is based on the premise that "analysis is not synthesis [and therefore], strategic planning is not strategy formulation" (p. 321). He further explains that no amount of elaboration will ever enable a formal process to take the place of managers and leaders who are fully engaged in their operations, or for that matter replace the critical and creative thinking that is necessary to create novel and innovative strategies. Mintzberg does not totally reject the use of strategic planning, but rather, he broadens the operational definition of the concept to include the intuitive thrust that other authors now include in their texts.

To summarize the Planning function, interdependency exists in the development and synchronization of the elements of the Planning process that includes the vision, mission, goals, objectives, and strategies. Second, the sole purpose of management is to focus the energies within an organization in order to achieve a common purpose. This purpose is normally formalized through the vision, mission statement, goals, and objectives of the organization. Although it is highly desirable that these forms of focus be formalized and made public to the individuals within an organization, their absence in writing does not mean that they do not exist. On the contrary, they live informally in the heads of the key decision makers in an organization and are revealed through their directions and task assignments. The lack of formal plans or having competing plans and operating systems in the organization usually is a critical obstacle for managers and leaders. It causes frictional turbulence to workers in different sections of the organization. Later it will be addressed why it plays a key role in separating the roles of managers and leaders and more importantly, how it affects the expectations that people have for these roles.

Organizing

The management function of organizing is more comprehensive than is generally understood. The short definition is "the process of arranging people and resources to work toward a common goal" (Schermerhorn, 1996). To better understand the concept that evolved from Fayol is to include the basic building blocks (systems) that will be required to build the structure that is needed to implement the plans at each level. As seen in Figure 2.7, these systems at a minimum involve:

- designing jobs
- grouping jobs
- establishing reporting relationships between jobs
- distributing authority among jobs
- coordinating activities between jobs
- differentiating between jobs.

Although this section is not designed to give an in-depth understanding of each of this function's subtopics, it should be noted that such topics as training, career development, and other human resource management topics fit

- **Organizational Design**
- **Staffing**
- **Reward/Promotional Systems**
- **Job Design**
- **Authority Policies**

Figure 2.7 The organizing function

within the conceptual framework of this function. As an example, to design a job, one must know the job specifications along with the skills required to accomplish this job. This leads to recruiting, training, and fostering career development in the organization.

As the mission statement changes, each organizational activity listed above needs to be revisited to determine whether the analysis, which resulted in how the organization was achieving the goals of the previous mission, is still applicable. In essence, organizers who do not consider the planning impact on the organizing function are doomed for failure.

In Figure 2.8, this interdependency of the management functions is illustrated. As painful and time-consuming as it may be to review all the systems in an organization, the lack of this effort can cause suboptimization as well as a loss of efficiency and effectiveness throughout the organization when new systems are added or older ones are adjusted. The lesson here is that each subsystem needs to be reviewed and adjusted as changes are made. Using Drucker's symphony analogy, parts of the organization will be on one sheet of music while others will be on another causing problems for the group as a whole.

The last subject to be discussed in this section is organizational design. Many organizations today were established during the Industrial Revolution movement where strict command and control relationships were the norm. Currently, there is a continuum of designs that are possible, as can be seen

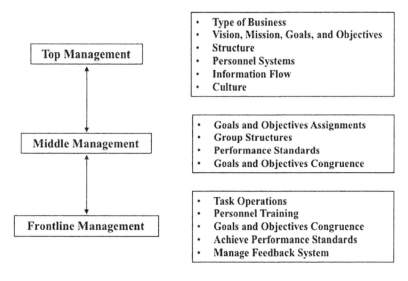

Figure 2.8 Organizational responsibilities

in Figure 2.9. What is even more daunting about this reality is that the way we view the world is inherent in our thought process, vocabulary, and the way we view work. As the world transitions from Toffler's pure Agriculture and Industrial Waves of existence, hybrid situations become the new norm. In other words, strains of behavior still live on in each wave but manifest themselves in ways that are interwoven into the ever-evolving world societies. From an organization development perspective, the strain of addressing each wave in new hybrid forms becomes challenging for managers and leaders in all organizations.

This range of organizational design shows not only a continuum of possibilities, it also indicates a temporal aspect, see Figure 2.9. What is shown at the left side of the illustration is the strict bureaucratic structure that was common during the strength of the Industrial Wave. Moving to the right side of the figure, a combination of various organizational forms that may be needed as the workplace evolves can be seen. These changes could be caused by an increase in the education of the workforce, the pace of competition requiring quicker decisions, and the need for more free-flowing input from others to elicit the optimum viable options in a timely basis. Although these are just a few of the factors pressuring organizations to evolve, it is an overwhelming task for managers and administrators to establish an organizational structure that will best use the talents of their workers in order to achieve organizational goals. This is especially true with today's workforce that identifies more with the High Tech/Info Age and less and less with the command-and-control philosophies of the Industrial Age.

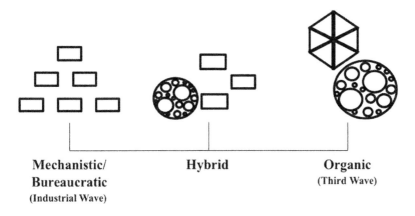

Mechanistic/   **Hybrid**   **Organic**
Bureaucratic   (Third Wave)
(Industrial Wave)

Figure 2.9 The continuum of organizational designs

Motivating

Of all the functions of management, motivating others is probably the most difficult to accomplish. Employee issues consume much of a manger's time. It is this function where an individual's value system bumps into organizational values. In Figure 2.10, we see that the Motivating function, as used in this text, includes activities that are dependent on the personal choices and characteristics of managers within the organization.

In the past during the Industrial Wave, workers were considered interchangeable parts. Although this is a sweeping generalization, and there certainly were recognized differences in talent and experience in the workplace, too many workers were put into a caste-type system that exists even in today's workplace. For example, blue-collar versus white-collar and college educated versus no college education. The point to be made is that in organizations today, we still have a worker caste system in place that challenges managers to use various motivational techniques in order to build a team effort to accomplish organizational goals.

The factors that shape worker motivation have been a hot topic of study and debate since the beginning of the Industrial Age. A watershed event in this field of endeavor occurred at the Hawthorne Plant of Western Electric in 1924. While researchers were conducting studies to determine a precise

* **Leadership Styles**
* **Motivational Techniques**
* **Group Dynamics**
* **Decision-Making Techniques**

Figure 2.10 The motivating function

relationship between illumination and individual efficiency, they discovered that regardless of the illumination level, worker productivity increased. At a loss to explain the rationale for these results, Elton Mayo, the renowned father of the Human Relations Movement, put a team together to study this phenomenon. We should remember that during this period of history, workers were generally considered to be an extension of the machinery. The underlying factor for this mentality seemed to be a culture of obedience; i.e., obedience to the head of the family, obedience to royalty or landowners, and lastly, obedience to some deity through a religious hierarchy. Even today, this scenario is being globally played out.

With this historical backdrop of obedience, Mayo's study found that people are not machines and that they can be motivated by understanding who they are as individuals. As a result, the Hawthorne Studies broadened the productivity factors from merely a technical and physical spectrum to a spectrum that included human behavior factors. In addition to the historical baggage of man's servitude in the workplace, Mayo put part of the blame of this limited view of man in the Industrial workplace on David Ricardo, a prominent British political economist from the late eighteenth century. Wren (1972) writes that Mayo "was concerned with the failure of social and political institutions to provide means for effective human collaboration in . . . mass producing society" (p. 293). In Mayo's view, the failure of human collaboration was influenced by Ricardo's interpretation of a society that was articulated in his Rabble Hypothesis. The Hypothesis' premises are:

- Natural society consists of a horde of unorganized individuals.
- Every individual acts in a manner calculated to secure his self-preservation and self-interest.
- Every individual thinks logically, to the best of their ability, in the service of this aim.

(Wren, p. 294)

Although Wren contends that Mayo may have read too much into Ricardo's Rabble Hypothesis, he conceded that Mayo was responsible for having the world "rethink its concepts of authority by abandoning the notion of unitary authority from a central head, be it state, the church, or the industrial leader" (Wren, p. 294). Mayo's Hawthorne studies clearly show that finding the right balance between task requirements and worker motivation is critical to the success of any organization. Although people like Abraham Maslow and Frederick Herzberg have tried to map out some type of topography that explains work motivation, most would agree that there exists a motivational hierarchy that, if tapped into properly, can enrich the work experience of individuals. As is usually the case in the practical world, designing such an organization proves more difficult than the theories imply.

To achieve a more enlightened understanding of motivation in the workplace, review of the literature reveals that there continues to be a strong effort involving this issue. It seems like every week a new management or leadership book hits the shelves from scholars, present and former business leaders, and former military leaders. With the abundance of these books, it is difficult for the public to sort through them to find the specific pearls of wisdom that they need for their situation. Unfortunately, there is no single answer for creating a successful organization. Figure 2.11 makes this point. Additionally, it helps promote a dialogue focused on a better understanding of the robustness and complexity of management.

With all the turmoil occurring throughout the world today, it is apparent that although the Industrial Age has brought unparalleled prosperity, the movement to the High Tech/Information Age seems to have shocked the world. Referring to our discussion on Toffler's trilogy on societal change, in his first book *Future Shock* (1970), he astutely titled Part 1 "The Death of Permanence." Toffler recognized the human condition, and the obvious notion that people resist change. Although in the past there always has been change, the rate of change was imperceptible. However, since the beginning

Figure 2.11 The book jungle

of the Industrial Age this has not been the case. Vernor Vinge in his paper "The Singularity" presented at a NASA conference and Raymond Kurzweil in his book *The Age of Spiritual Machines: When Computers Exceed Human Intelligence* contributed to the mindset that change is happening at an exponential pace. Thus, as the complexity of the future comes upon us at an increasing speed, we need to pause and reflect on the worthy contributions of past writers concerning management and organizations.

In conclusion, there is no longer any doubt that the Internet has changed the workplace and our daily lives. Consequently, people in all facets of organizations are forced to adapt to a future that challenges managers and leaders to motivate their workers in order to assist them in developing responsive learning organizations that can compete in the world marketplaces while holding onto their values and credible past practices.

Controlling

This is probably the most misunderstood concept of the entire Management process. The word itself has come to be considered pejorative. It conjures up visions of bureaucratic control with everyone following strict procedures in the workplace. The real purpose of this concept, however, is to recognize that once the plan is in motion, there needs to be a mechanism to check the progress of the plan. Plans should not be fixed, regimented documents. They should be regarded as the best plan of action at a point in time, and yet able to be changed as the situation dictates. This does not mean a continual changing of the plan, but merely a plan that is flexible enough that when the execution of the plan falls outside the parameters laid out in the plan, appropriate managers need to be alerted in order to take the necessary corrective action. Thus, the controlling function becomes the thermometer that gauges the health of the organization as various plans are executed.

Some of the key factors of this function are seen in Figure 2.12. In the Planning process, the concept of how the execution of the plan will be monitored to meet specified parameters needs to be articulated. This monitoring could take place through timely reports flowing to decision makers, or through specified meetings to get key information to managers. It also should be specified where the decision makers will be located throughout the organization. Additionally, clarification and allocation of both the responsibilities and authority these decision makers have should be communicated throughout the organization.

In regard to the selection of the appropriate control measures, here are some factors that need to be considered:

- manager style
- tasks to be accomplished

- costs/criticality of activity
- expertise of the workforce
- general organizational climate.

Lastly, the distinction between an Information System and a Management Information System (MIS) should be made clear. An 'Information System' is a broad term used to collect, organize, and distribute information in an organization. Although there are many subsets to this system, the MIS is a subset system specifically designed to flow key information to decision makers. It is a control measure in Management to ensure that the right person gets the right information at the right time. It also includes ensuring that people do not get information overload. Review of the literature reveals that those organizations that are managed and led well are those organizations that are monitored on an appropriate basis. This allows decision makers to react in sufficient time to maintain the viability of the organization as well as controlling the flow of information in their respective organization.

A final note about the Management process should be stressed. All organizations use some form of this process be it an informal family unit or a multinational organization. The lack of a formally published process should not lead one to believe that a process is not actively being implemented. It is the analytical process we as humans go through while participating in collective activities. Even the seemingly random and out-of-control activities

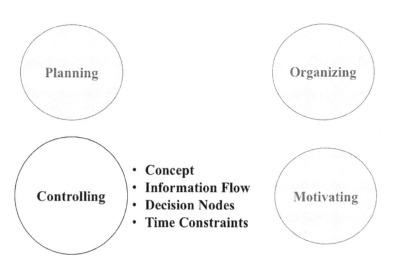

Figure 2.12 The controlling function

exhibited in this process either by a very loose process or the minds of decision makers can be traced back to a particular process. When this process is happening internally by an individual, it may be occurring almost instantaneously due to a previously learned mental process. In either case, the salient points are:

- The Management process is a universal process in group endeavors.
- The functions of the Management process are interdependent to one another.
- The Management process needs to find the balance between a formal process that focuses the energy of an organization while being able to adapt to the changing environment.

Now that the groundwork has been laid for how the POMC process evolved from Fayol's fourteen principles used by successful organizations, the term 'POMC model' will be used to analyze the evolution of this process over time. This analysis will enhance the readers' understanding of the robustness of the management concept as well as set the stage for its differentiation from the concept of leadership.

3 The evolution of the management process

Overview

At this point in the book we now ready to discuss the evolution of the management process, namely, the POMC model. By now, the reader should have an appreciation that organizations are living organisms. Although the constructs of an organization are continually changing, the basic management process still exists. All organizations plan, organize, motivate workers, and control organizational systems in order to achieve the mission, goals, and objectives. This is universally true regardless if it is not formally stated. Second, the functions (POMC) of the management process are intrinsically linked in that changing one function invariably affects the other functions.

The POMC timeline

Using the backdrop of the Management process, the stage is now set up to address the intricate interconnectedness of the process over time. To set the tone for this interconnectedness, a moving circle is illustrated. The circle represents an organization and the planning, organizing, motivating, and controlling (POMC) process it uses to accomplish its goals. It is the POMC model. In Figure 3.1, the circles are labeled "A" through "Z." This illustrates that the POMC process and its subsequent subsystems evolve over time. To realize the magnitude of this endeavor, Figure 2.8, "Organizational responsibilities," is superimposed on the Figure 3.2 POMC timeline. This can be seen in Figure 3.3. The point here is that inside each circle, all the systems of the POMC process are occurring. More importantly, it needs to be stressed that for each circle, all the POMC systems have been instituted at a different point on the timeline and under different conditions. When any changes are made to any part of the POMC process due to current and projected situations, all the systems involved within the POMC model need to be revisited to ensure that they are consistent with the new changes. If this does not occur, different parts of the process will be aligned with outdated systems that no longer reinforce the new direction of the organization.

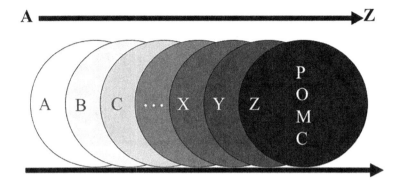

Figure 3.1   The POMC timeline

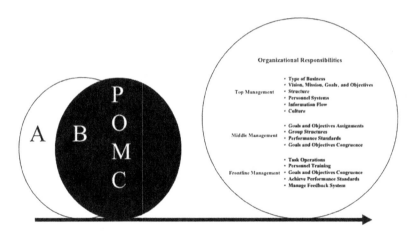

Figure 3.2   Detailed POMC model

As an example, new organizational plans may call for workers with different skills sets but hiring, promotion, and incentive guidelines were not changed appropriately. In another case, inventory levels have been changed but logistical supports systems were not adequately addressed to count for this last change to the POMC process. Time-consuming, yes, but a necessity in order to preclude coordination gaps and to ensure that the necessary adjustments are made so that all the energies of the organization are working effectively together toward the same objective.

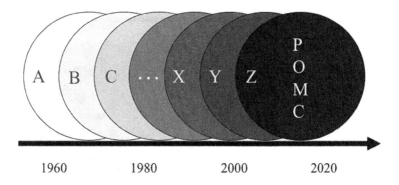

Figure 3.3 Organization development

Organizational change processes

Long-term, continuous adjustments are needed to fine-tune an organization. Review of the literature reveals that there are two general categories of organizational change. They are Organization Development (OD) and Organization Transformation (OT). According to Porras and Silvers (1991), OD is

> a set of behavioral science theories, values, strategies, and techniques aimed at the planned change of organizational work settings creating a better fit between the organization's capabilities and its current environmental demands. The purpose of OD is to promote changes that help the organization better address predicted future environments.
>
> (p. 289)

Organizational Transformation has the same purpose but the phrase "promoting paradigmatic change" is the defining difference between the two terms (p. 289).

To underscore the difference between OT and OD, Figure 3.4 shows an orderly progress to the future by fine-tuning an organization as it stays within the traditional philosophies and practices of competing in the marketplace. The key here is using OD techniques to fine-tune the traditional way of doing business.

Unfortunately, organizations stay too long with their current POMC model causing a gap to occur in the natural evolution of the POMC process. In reviewing the distinctions between OD and OT, the major factor

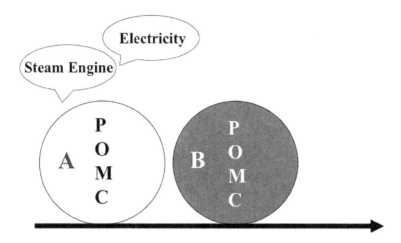

Figure 3.4   Organizational transformation

is whether an organization is merely updating plans and operating systems at each level of the organization within guidelines of its current vision and corporate culture, or whether the organization is moving drastically away to a new vision and requires a new mindset. Change in any form is typically stressful in any organization, but OT tends to shock the system. As a result, it requires careful leadership and management efforts to ensure that the energies unleashed by restructuring are refocused to support the implementation of the new vision, that is, a new strategic plan. This includes the critical areas of the creation of new responsibilities, authority relationships, and most importantly, expectations of employees throughout the organization.

In his book *Innovator's Dilemma*, Clayton Christensen (1997) writes about the problem of transitioning from OD to OT. In overview, he explains that when successful organizations have a winning formula with their product or service, it becomes difficult for them to adjust to the next invention that will affect their position in the marketplace. Think about it, the organization views the marketplace in a specific way, they plan a specific way, they operate and hire workers a specific way, and each of these ways is geared toward the marketplace where the organization has been successful. When a new invention or new process comes along that challenges an organization's practices, the resistance to change is so overwhelming that organizations usually stay within the parameters that brought them success in the past rather than generate a transformation that may or may not keep them competitive. An easy way to think about the magnitude of the change is to recall a time in one's life when you had to rethink how you act or view the world. Some examples may be:

- graduating from school
- establishing personal independence
- getting married
- becoming a parent.

For many of us, it is terrifying to enter a world where our former way of operating is no longer productive or appropriate. High levels of anxiety are the norm whether we are talking about individuals or organizations. Figure 3.5 shows a concrete example of when the world evolved from steam engines to electricity. One can imagine the infrastructure that was set up for the use of steam engines throughout the Industrial world. The onset of electrical power totally transformed how companies did business. Companies that lagged behind in making the change to electricity often had difficulty recovering from their resistance. On the other hand, companies that missed new trends could attempt to leap frog their competitors and get to the next trend first. Of course, this is a tremendous risk, but it may be better than playing catch up by retooling their organization only to find that the next

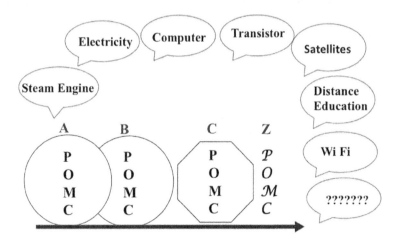

Figure 3.5 Organizational transformation events

invention is already upon them. Evidently, the caveat here is that there exist factors that influence the ability of the organization to hold on for the next opportunity. Some of these factors are type of industry, flexibility of its infrastructure and people, and the strength of its resources.

Illustrated in Figure 3.5 are some probable factors that have caused OT stress for many organizations. As you can imagine these major inventions or world events have not only impacted organizations throughout the world but also have affected the world economies and the way we live our daily lives. Furthermore, the design has been changed in configuration "C" from a circle to an octagon. The reason for the change is to make the point that organizational designs for the future may not be those that are traditionally used, especially from an Industrial Age mentality. These are likely organizations that have yet to be designed.

Chaordic Age

For the configuration labeled "Z" in Figure 3.5, we give a tip of our hat to an old acquaintance, Dee Hock, former CEO of VISA. Hock coined the term 'chaordic' that is derived from two words, 'chaos' and 'order.' In his book, *Birth of the Chaordic Age* (1999), he lays out the plight of organizations when he says:

> Poised as we are on the knife's edge between socio-environmental disaster and a livable future, one question cuts to the core of our future: Will the result be chaos and the even more repressive and dictatorial regimes so often arising from chaotic conditions? Or will we emerge from the eggshell of our Industrial Age institutions into a new world of profound, constructive organizational change?
>
> (Hock, 1999, p. 6)

Hock believed that the organization of the future would have the characteristics "of community based on shared purpose calling to the higher aspirations of people" (p. 6). Who knows what this organization will look like, thus the lack of design in position "Z." The issue of chaos as it applies to organizations will be discussed in Chapter 6.

Much has been written about self-organizing systems as we search for a way to deal with the pace of organizational evolution combined with the exponential flow of information. Regardless of the pace of change, the POMC process will still occur, be it formally in writing or through a mental process by decision makers. Unfortunately, due to the speed in which decisions are sometimes made, unintended consequences may occur because of the lack of attention to key factors or worse yet, an underappreciation of the POMC process that is always in play.

A final comment

The message in this chapter is a "blinding flash of the obvious"; namely, that an organization is made of people, not just things or processes. As obvious as this may be, when one studies how organizations design jobs and the structures within our organizations, one wonders whether this message is really that obvious. As individuals in organizations employ the management process to achieve the stated mission, the realization needs to be that when the mission changes, corresponding changes (ripples) occur throughout the organization. Some people call them second-order and third-order effects, which these are, but be aware that like a pond, the ripple continues through each level and each person of the organization. Some effects may not be large enough to be classified as second-order and third-order effects, but they are always present. These effects are there because the organization is, and always has been, a living organism that is an open system.

Regarding the Management Process (POMC model), there are several key points that should be remembered:

- The Management Process is a universal process that applies to all organizations whether formal or informal.
- Management is a discipline whose knowledge base continues to evolve. There are no magic formulas to solve organizational problems. The crucial factor in solving organizational problems is critical thinking.
- The organization is a living organism where changes affect all its systems. As a result, each system needs to be revisited as alterations are made to ensure that each process continues to support these changes.
- The POMC model is a moving train that seeks to vision the future while anchoring the present.

4 The struggle to define leadership

Overview

In management, key concepts seem to overlap. Since the concepts of management and leadership are two such concepts, the previous chapters were presented in order to lay the foundation to address this overlap. As a result, once this distinction is presented between these concepts, it will be useful to managers and leaders as analytical tools in their decision-making process. With this wedge driven between these concepts, the following chapters will tackle why this is an important issue and not just a semantic drill.

Almost every day, whether it be in business, government, or even sports, we hear the word 'leader' thrown around. It is tossed around so loosely that the word starts to lose its meaning. In business, for example, the top executives or managers of an organization are usually referred to as the leaders of the organization. In government, the president, governor, and mayor are given the same accolade. It seems that their official titles are not a sufficient descriptor for the person. In sports, it is even worse since the leading scorer is often named the 'leader' of the team. This is evident in American football when a quarterback is usually not considered great on athletic merit alone but is great only when taking on the burden of being the emotional leader of the team as well.

We think most would agree that the concept of leader is intrinsically valued by society. The problem arises when the title is bestowed loosely on individuals who may not possess leadership qualities. This can become damaging to the individual and their organization in the long run. So often we see experts in an organization promoted to management because of their excellent job performance, or because of personal relationships with key executives. With nepotism alive and well in all types of organizations, these organizations often get a manager and lose an expert worker.

The bottom line is that everyone is not capable of being a manager, let alone a leader. Certainly, they can be designated as manager but at what costs? This is the crux of the question being addressed in this publication. To start, what are the differences?

Management versus leadership

By now most of us are getting tired of the endless attempts to distinguish between the concepts of manager and leader. Some people have given up and use the terms interchangeably. A review of the literature reveals that there is a wide array of viewpoints on the issue. As an example, the U.S. Army includes the concept of management as part of its concept of leadership, while others like Griffin (2013) and Schermerhorn (2005) include leadership as a major function of management.

As stated in the Introduction, the simple experiment Robert conducted at a conference in Budapest and later in his classes shows that confusion exists between the concepts of leading and managing. Why the wide divergence in positions? Why does the U.S. Army use leadership as the focal point while the business world and academe take a totally opposite perspective? A more important question may be "What difference does it make, as long as the organization accomplishes its goals and objectives?"

The answer to this question lies in the fact that there continues to be a myriad of management 'how to' books published every year which is an undeniable indicator that there is an unquenchable thirst to find a quick and easy solution that will solve organizational problems. The answer also lies in the apparent intrinsic feeling that the long-term health of the organization depends on both management and leadership, even though many have a difficult time in separating them conceptually.

To address this issue, Figure 4.1 presents a visual representation of a wedge to separate these concepts. The basic premise for this illustration is that the boundaries between managers and leaders rest with the derivation of authority for the manager and the leader. For managers, the authority is derived from the organization, while for leaders it springs from the unfettered willingness of the people to follow. In the case of managers, including military commanders, their authority rests with the legal status of their position. Since there is a contractual arrangement between the employees and the organization, employees are willing to comply with organizational regulations and procedures and comply with the direction of a duly authorized person. Under these conditions, employees have agreed to comply with official, directed goals. But, and this is a very big 'but,' because when most employees strive to attain organizational goals, they may only be complying because they are contractually required to and not because they buy into the action being directed by supervisors. In other words, the employee may be externally committed, but may not have internalized the goals as part of their value systems.

When employees do internalize organizational goals as a part of their own value system (private acceptance), the individual who influenced them

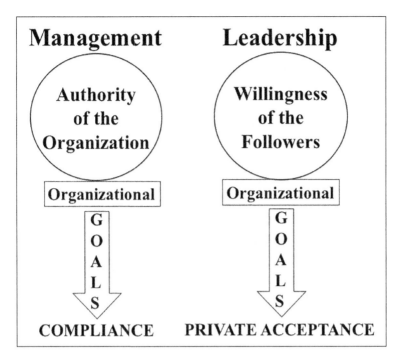

Figure 4.1   Management versus leadership

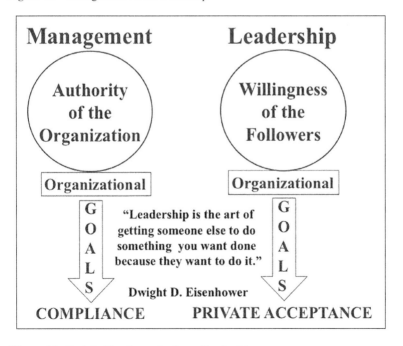

Figure 4.2   Dwight Eisenhower's view of leadership

to do so has become their leader. The key point is that managers and leaders both use the management process to achieve organizational goals regardless of how their authority is obtained. Essentially, the manager is using organizational authority to focus the energies of employees in order to achieve organizational goals while the leader goes a step beyond by getting employees to embrace the goals as a part of their own value systems.

Figure 4.2 shows that the discovery and insight between leader and manager is not original in that former president and five-star general Dwight D. Eisenhower already nailed down the difference.

A systems view of organizations

Now that we have a distinction between manager and leader, the realistic question becomes "How do you know when a person is really the leader in the eye of the employees?" Just performing the task assigned by the organization may not be the best indicator to determine the answer to this question. To address this, we need to view the factors that motivate employee actions. More specifically, we need to use a system's perspective. Figure 4.3 is a visual that portrays some variables that affect human behavior in organizations. Using the Venn diagram, three major factors are illustrated that influence employee behavior in organizations. Circle A depicts the influence of the leader, while Circle B depicts the influences of organizational infrastructure, including management style, organizational design,

A - **Leadership**

B - **Organizational
    Factors**

   · **Structure**
   · **Management
      style**
   · **Systems**
   · **Climate**

C - **Socialization**

U - **Organization**

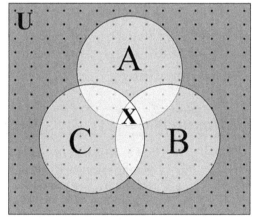

© 1974, R. Murphy

Figure 4.3 A systems view of organizations

task specification, incentive systems, and organizational climate and culture. Circle C reflects the individual's own socialization 'baggage' that includes personal traits from their upbringing, schooling, and general life experiences. The letter "U" represents the organization environment while the series of dots represent possible actions by an employee (Bonvillian and Murphy, 1996, pp. 192–194). Figure 4.3 demonstrates that a person's actions may be the result of any one – or even all – of the major factors. So, when good work is being accomplished in an organization, it may be the result of three major factors: (1) good leadership, (2) good people who have been instilled with solid work ethics, and (3) a good organization that has a corporate culture of fair and equitable practices. Ideally reaching the X place in the diagram where all three factors are at play is the ideal but sadly, it is not the norm. Determining who is a really a leader is a longitudinal question. What this means is that immediate responses by employees may just be a reaction to current stress factors of the situation. Such factors can include peer pressure, fear of reprisal by legitimate authority, or reflexive responses that are not well thought out. To determine the core value of individuals, what is needed is an analysis of long-term employee behavior. Specifically, do people achieve organizational goals primarily due to organizational pressures (reward and punishment) or because a leader has influenced their value system?

This is a good place to stress that an organization's leaders may not be those who are formally designated by the organization. The leader could be anyone in the organization who is well respected by others to the point that their actions, be it deeds or words, influence the value system of others. Second, leadership is not based on the worthiness of the leader's deeds but rather on whether people internalize the leader's influence. Regardless of which notorious person you want to use as an example, if they influenced people to internalize their deeds or words, they are leaders.

A final comment

This chapter was designed to place a definitive wedge between the concepts of manager and leader. Managing is not just an exercise to control objects and processes. It also includes the efforts to motivate people to achieve organizational goals. Leading within the context of an organization is about having employees internalize organizational goals. In overview, this means that organizations need to guide their employees to work toward these goals because they sincerely believe in them to the point that incentives and repercussions are not the driving force for achieving organizational goals but rather their internal value system. This does not mean that employees do not desire incentives but rather that they have made the goals a part of their value system. According to Wren (1972), accomplishing these goals also enables them to fulfill their self-actualizing needs in Maslow's Hierarchy of Needs Model (p. 328).

Lastly, it should be stressed that both leaders and managers should be focused on attaining organizational goals. To this end, if the leadership skills are lacking or missing in the duly appointed managers, the fallback position for them is the authority invested in them by the organization. Normally this type of environment is not as efficient and effective as a leader-led organization but it should be sufficient to maintain the health of the organization. The natural fallout from these types of organizations is that more incentives are needed or force imposed to get people to achieve organizational goals.

5 Why the difference matters

Overview

Before we address the question of why the differences between manager and leader are important, a review of what has been discussed so far is necessary. In Chapter 1, Toffler's concept of how society has evolved to stay abreast of the ever-changing landscape of innovations that impact on how humans work and live was introduced. The reality is that we are always steeped in organizational change when studying human group behavior. The challenge is to balance the valuable lessons humanity has learned throughout the ages with the opportunities afforded to those through recent developments and new innovations.

With Chapter 2, the goal was to give a sense of the journey that the evolution of management thought has taken. Like other disciplines, many scholars and practitioners have added to the field of knowledge, we hope, for the best. However, unlike other fields of study, management knowledge is with us ubiquitously. Additionally, due to the explosion of communication sources today, the addition to the management information base is exponential. Notice that the word 'knowledge' base was not used. The reason is that general information needs to be vetted through some process that verifies that the information is both valid and worthy of being added to the knowledge base. In academe, information in the form of theories, studies, presentations are presented to a body of experts who have the responsibility of giving their stamp of approval that this new information is valid and reliable knowledge. This is where the distinction between information and knowledge lies. Unfortunately, because of the abundance of information flowing throughout our society, this formal vetting process rarely takes place and depends on each individual to determine the validity and reliability of the information. Just watching news programs with their series of experts on both sides of the issue dramatically demonstrates this frustrating and challenging task.

This text is not necessarily intended to be a replacement for a basic management or leadership text that is traditionally found on today's campuses or in bookstores. What is presented, however, are the building blocks needed to build a foundation in order to broaden an understanding of the field of management. This effort is further needed to counterbalance a realistic view of leadership.

The challenge faced in Chapter 3 was to give a visual of the Management Process as an evolutionary process. Many of the managers that the authors engaged with over the past forty years admitted that they have the requisite plans that most organizations have but when these managers were pinned down on the execution of these plans, they confessed that the written plans usually just sat on the shelf. This all-too-common situation led the authors to illustrate how the Management Process (POMC) is affected over time. This evolution of the POMC process becomes important in this chapter when we delve into why the difference between manager and leader really matters and why understanding the difference is important.

Chapter 4 was the definitive effort to drive a wedge between the concepts of manager and leader. The purpose of this chapter is to explain why this distinction is important and how it affects the operation and growth of an organization.

Leadership situations

While addressing the difference between manager and leader, it became apparent that an analysis was needed to demonstrate the ways in which people use the word 'leader.' In doing so, it was determined that the use of the word 'leading' seems to be so pervasive in our everyday language that its meaning is adrift in the different sectors of society. This analysis begins with addressing the specific categories as to how the word 'leader' was used.

Figure 4.3 illustrates the four major situations where the word 'leader' is used. In both the *First to Act* and *Best at a Skill* situation, it seems appropriate to use the word 'leader,' especially for the second situation. In the second situation, it seems reasonable to have skilled individuals influence others in the group particularly when it involves skills germane to the group's mission. There are various examples from sports to work environments where highly skilled individuals are expected to inspire others with good habits that will result in better goal attainment for the group as a whole. In these two situations, the use of the word 'leader' is valid in a limited sense but does not encompass what can be considered the fullest meaning of the term 'leader.'

The most common usage of the word 'leading' is when someone is the first person to perform an action. By default, these individuals are said to be in the lead or are the leader. Although this is an obvious example when used in this sense, people are not embracing the full meaning of the word 'leader.' In fact, this definition is merely a reaction to the act of someone being first. Having said that, we are sure there are occasions when people who are first to act influence the value system of others but this is probably an exception rather than the rule.

In the second situation, *Best at a Skill*, someone is called 'leader' when the individual is the best at some activity like sales, a sport, or some other endeavor. Although this is another valid use of the word 'leader,' it also does not capture the full meaning of the concept of leader. For example, in an organizational setting, being named a leader raises others' expectations of what they can possibly deliver. In fact, it almost becomes a halo effect in that a top performer is expected to translate their special skills into actions of inspiring and leading those around them. This scenario plays itself out in the workplace where top performers are promoted to key management positions, which result in the loss of a top performer and the entrenching of a weak manager with little or no leadership potential. This occurs because most organizations do not have an infrastructure that rewards top perform-ers except through the management chain. They confuse the skills of a top performer with the skills necessary to manage people or worse yet, with the attributes, skills, and management potential needed to lead them.

In the case of the third situation, *Head of an Organization*, labeling man-agers throughout the organization as leaders is a problem. First, placing managers at appropriate levels in the organization based on their skill level is critical to maintaining the viability of the organization. To automatically call them leaders, however, usually bestows upon them the baggage of expec-tations reserved for leaders. These expectations are normally expectations reserved for leaders, which are far different from those that are bestowed on managers. Specifically, the expectation that these newly selected manag-ers will in fact be leaders who can inspire employees to internalization of the vision, policies, and culture of the organization is not always a realis-tic situation. Although it is extremely difficult to identify those individuals who have the potential to be organizational leaders and those who do not, it should be recognized that many of the people who have worked their way up through the organization are probably very good managers and are a real value to the organization and deserve to be there. Unfortunately, what peo-ple want is a great manager and by extension a great leader.

In Figure 5.1, an *Organizational Leader* is placed at the top. In this position, the person who is a true leader, not just in name but rather through their effect on those around them, is someone who can get people to internally embrace the organization's vision, policies, and corporate culture. The manager's domain is based on a contractual arrangement between employees and the organization where the manager is the duly

Figure 5.1 Types of leading situations

appointed organizational representative. Although employees are legally bound, they may or may not privately accept the values, vision, policies, and corporate culture of the organization. This is not a bad situation but rather it is the minimal level of cooperation needed for a healthy work environment. In essence, the workers may not totally agree with everything espoused by the organization, but it is acceptable to a worker's value system. That is, as long as the organization provides the necessary incentive, or unfortunately, organizational punishment. In this instance, the incentive and/or punishment is the driving force for the employees, not the internal commitment.

Two more important points need to be addressed before continuing on. First, being a leader or manager is not an 'all or nothing' scenario. Depending on a number of factors including task, condition, and standards, or whether someone is just a manager or in fact a leader should be seen as a fluid situation. More correctly, being a manager is always a fixed reality whereas being a leader is a moving target. To visualize this, a review of Figure 4.3, here listed as Figure 5.2, will help.

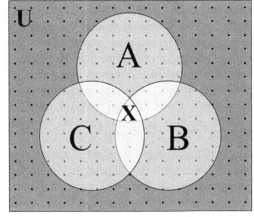

A - Leadership

B - Organizational
    Factors

   · Structure
   · Management
     style
   · Systems
   · Climate

C - Socialization

U - Organization

© 1974, R. Murphy

Figure 5.2 A systems view of organizations

In Figure 5.2, remember the dots represent possible courses of action people take in an organization. Thus 'U' represents the organization's universe of actions. Now, the question we addressed earlier was what factors influenced individual actions in an organizational environment. It was expressed that the three circles of the Venn diagram were the macro reasons that influence a person's action. Without getting too complicated on the factors that influence individual behavior, it can be seen that there are actions influenced by leaders, Circle A, by managers, Circle B, and by a person's upbringing, Circle C. All affect individuals, creating a complex web of reasons why they make the choices they do. The ideal zone is area X, where all influencing behaviors come together. Figure 5.2 also considers that there are unknown actions, black dots, which are not contained in one of the circles. The reality is that there may be other reasons for a person's action that cause the person to act in a particular way.

The difference matters

Since the word 'leader' is so infused in our daily vocabulary, it is difficult to find a replacement word. It continues to beg the question, "Does it make a difference?" The unequivocal answer is *yes*, it does. When we talk about an organizational scenario where certain people control and influence others in a group, especially in a formal setting, it is crucial to have a thorough understanding of terms used in association with individuals throughout an organization. That is why in Figure 5.1, other categories of leading have been separated out in order to highlight the distinction of Organization Leader versus other forms of leadership. The answer to why it makes a difference lies in the baggage that the concepts of manager and leader carry. The baggage referenced is baggage that feeds into the emotions and expectations of prospective followers that can ultimately weigh on the success of an organization whether positively or negatively.

Examples of this can be observed every day in newspapers and on television where CEOs of large companies, religious hierarchies, university presidents, or even political figures do not meet the worker's or public's expectations of what a leader should be doing. It is apparent that people cannot just call these people 'manager,' 'administrator,' and 'commander' or by whatever official title they may hold. It seems that the default title for those in charge is leader. In line with Figure 5.1, it is the authors' position that only those who influence people to adjust their value system should be called a leader. Until it is apparent that followers have internalized the proposed leader's influence, it is uncertain which factor(s) presented in Figure 5.2 prompted a person to act. It seems like the old adage of "if no one is following, no one is leading" has some truth to it. To be more accurate in this adage, "if people are not influenced to internalize the message of the purported leader, no one is leading." We know there can be an argument as to the difference between a change agent and a leader but we take the position that leaders are change agents while all change agents may not be leaders.

This is not a book on how-to guide on ways to become a manager or leader; it is an attempt to show the differences of these two concepts in order to guide readers to a more thorough understanding of the domain of each of these terms. With this deeper understanding, more realistic expectations can be incorporated into daily tasks as well as the various plans an organization has. Because the concept of manager has taken on such a pejorative connotation in our society, many people automatically exchange the word 'leader' for anyone in charge of a group. For example, in academe and other non-profit organizations the term 'administrator' is used. In the military, the word 'leader' is preferred. Unfortunately, only in the for-profit world is the word 'manager' commonly used. The exception is when top performers and inspirational managers are referred to as leaders. To address the magnitude of why this difference is important, we need to understand its effect on the Organizational Change process.

The difference impacts organizational change

Two realties exist when addressing organizational change. First, "What do we change?" and second, "How do we get the people in the organization to change?" Although there are many excellent techniques cited in various literary efforts to help focus the change process, before organizational change is attempted, there must exist a reasonable sense of where to take the organization. This includes both the overall direction as well as how to restructure the energies of the organization. The first question is appropriate when working through a Strategic Planning process in order to derive an organization's vision, mission, goals, and objectives. To do this, the question, "Why the distinction between manager and leader matters?" comes into play.

To display the difference between managers and leaders, Figure 5.3 demonstrates a way to show how a manager and leader affect the organization. In Figure 5.3, the iceberg represents the organization and all its activities. When changes occur, many of the actions taken by the organization to affect the desired change are surface changes. These surface-type changes have less emotional drain on the employees as compared to other changes that could be made.

These are changes that managers – through their organizational authority – can easily direct people to comply with while getting little employee resistance. Chester Barnard, the executive scholar of the early twentieth century, developed the concept of "zone of indifference" (Wren, 1972 p. 316). According to Bernard, this is a zone where employees take orders without resisting the authority of the person giving the order. However, this is not the case with more drastic changes that may affect an employee's deep personal values. Getting people to accept drastic change usually requires the

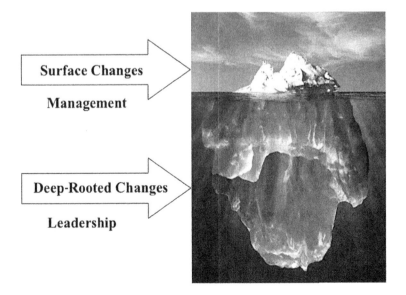

Figure 5.3 The Organization Iceberg Change Model

touch of a leader, namely, someone who can get individuals to 'buy in' to deep-rooted changes as well to accept the circumstances and situation at hand. Examples of some specific organizational actions and their possible effect on the employee are seen in Figure 5.4. In this diagram, as the organizational action becomes directly in conflict with the employee's value system, the more concerned and conflicted the employee becomes. As this situation challenges the traditional values of an organization, it becomes more apparent that the organization may be undergoing an Organizational Transformation.

To emphasize the point of the need to understand the difference between manager and leader, in Figure 5.5 the iceberg has been superimposed to visually show surface-type changes versus deep-rooted changes. This illustration stresses the point that the deeper and more complex the changes, the greater the need for strong transformational leaders.

With this split in the identity of manager and leader, it becomes easier to see why frustration occurs in workers, as expected results are not received from managers or the supposed leaders. The rationale for this frustration lies in the expectation framework people have for managers and leaders.

As shown in Figure 5.6, managers are more successful at surface-type issues while leaders are needed for deeper-rooted issues. When there is no distinction between these two entities, the expectations placed on leaders are projected onto managers. This does not mean that managers cannot solve

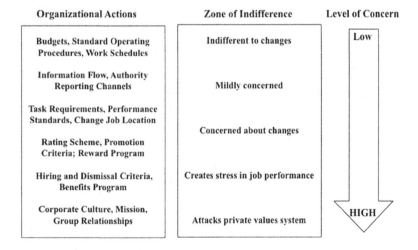

Figure 5.4 Organizational actions that affect individuals

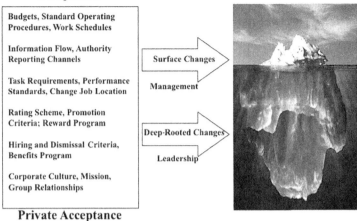

Figure 5.5 Organizational actions with Iceberg

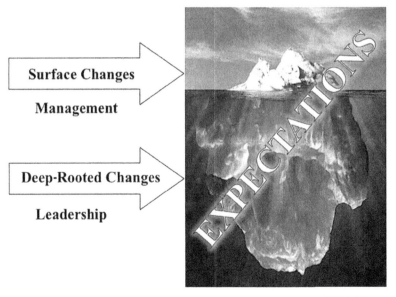

Figure 5.6 Iceberg with expectations

deep-rooted issues but rather to do so, these individuals need to depend more on the reward and punishment systems to obtain their desired results. Generally, people comply with very emotional changes if the rewards or punishments are sufficient to deal with the stress resulting from deep-rooted changes. A major drawback to using reward and punishment systems is that compliance is normally short-lived and requires constant replenishment. The best solution is to have leaders influencing those changes in order to get employees to buy in to the point that it becomes a part of their internal value system. This is the preferred journey toward a long-term solution.

It is very difficult to discern who is a leader and who is merely a top performer. We have a difficult time separating top performers from those individuals who inspire others to change their personal value system. Additionally, just because an individual may be a leader in one situation or at one level of the organization does not necessarily indicate that their leadership abilities are viable at higher levels of the organization, and actual leadership abilities are difficult to identify until the moment arises for the person to utilize those skills. Being the smartest, most athletic, or most likeable person may not be sufficient for that person to become a leader within the organization. These are all desirable qualities, as shown in the *Great Man* theories (Stogdill, 1974, pp. 17–18) of leadership but depending on the dynamics of one's organization, many other factors may, and often do, come into play.

Although we often joke about how certain bosses got promoted, Lawrence Peter and Raymond Hull wrote the book *The Peter Principle* (1969) to specifically address this question. *The Peter Principle* infers that people are promoted until they reach a level of incompetence. This is a result of the assessment of a person's ability to perform at the next level of an organization based upon their performance in their current position. If this is not difficult enough, it becomes even more complicated considering that it is very difficult in the short run to distinguish between who is a manager and who is really a leader. This difficulty is compounded in organizations that require managers and potential leaders to move on, often limiting their time to build relationships with their subordinates.

While Robert was teaching senior military and government civilians, Figure 5.7 was used to address the domains of leaders and managers at different levels of the organization. The focus was to characterize the different levels of an organization in such a way as to address the skills needed at each of these levels. On the X axis, there are specified organizational positions. At the extreme left, you have frontline managers and their equivalent in various types of organizations. As you move toward the right along the X axis you see positions of increasing responsibility and authority. On the Y axis, the degree of certainty and complexity that managers and leaders

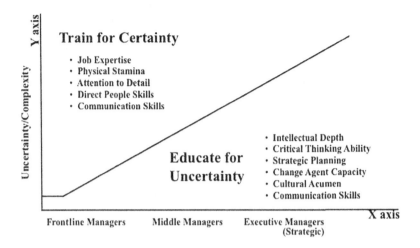

Figure 5.7 The changing organizational landscape

cope with in their respective positions is illustrated. Although absolute certainty is not realistic, the extreme left of the illustration reflects organizational jobs that are more straightforward and follow Standard Operating Procedures (SOPs). In essence, they are jobs that require people to be trained to specific standards. Moving to the right of the graph, the jobs involve more ambiguity where critical thinking skills become more valued in order to maintain the viability of the organization, especially during transformational times. This situation is a great example of the Toffler affect, that is, moving from an Industrial Age mentality to his Third Wave mentality where evolving technology and information flows dictate organizational survivability.

The graph in Figure 5.7 is helpful for several reasons. First, it makes the point that employees are trained for certainty and educated to handle complex uncertain events. It is also the case that individuals who lead at lower levels of the organization may need a more structured environment to be a viable frontline leader or manager.

Second, in viewing the center diagonal line of the graph, it can be seen that as an individual moves up the organization, moving to the right on the graph, less certainty exists requiring repetitive actions where Standard Operating Procedures (SOPs) are applicable. At higher levels of the organization where the issues are more complex, the use of SOPs is limited and the need for policy guidelines are increasingly necessary.

An interesting change was made from the draft version of this graph. You will note that there is white area at the far lower left of the graph. Initially, the diagonal line that separated training versus educating arenas evenly divided the graph, thus making each area theoretically equal. In discussions at the Army War College, there was a realization that media coverage, as well as the advances in social networking and actions of workers at frontline levels, could have serious strategic impacts on an organization. As a result, the world of certainty is challenged, thereby making it necessary that all employees be educated to some extent on complex issues that do not have easy ready-made answers. This becomes a vexing issue to get employees to understand the sensitivity of company policies and goals. However, this gives way to potential whistleblowing and the potential for company secrets to be exposed. The issues concerning whistleblowing are beyond the scope of this book, but understanding what you can expect from a leader's influence versus a manager's mandate has a greater chance of having employees form a better bond with the organization.

In conclusion, the default position in all organizations should not be that all managers are also leaders. Second, regardless of the type of organization, the POMC model is the underlining process from which to plan, control, and change an organization. Understanding the depth and breadth of this process and the necessary changes that must take place to evolve it as needed should be the focus of everyone in the organization. Also, it should be remembered that all organizations are extensions of their members and therefore are living organisms. Change is inevitable, as is the need to maintain the values that make an organization viable and relevant.

6 Future challenges for managers and leaders

As a general policy, defying the reality of change isn't a wise thing to do. Most people would agree that being ready for change is not being ready; but, apparently, being ready isn't easy. Being ready takes time, energy, and effort; and even more, it takes confronting our fear of change, our hate for what it does to our lives. Increasing organizational flexibility begins at a personal level . . . but it must end as an organizational act.

William A. Pasmore
(Creating Strategic Change, 1994, p. 270)

Sorting out the future

No one can accurately predict what tomorrow will bring. Volatility, uncertainty, complexity, and ambiguity will define our future work environment. Some change patterns will be discontinuous and hard to identify and frustration will be the norm for those who expect to control the future. Drucker (1994) summed up this pent-up frustration in writing "One cannot manage change. One can only be ahead of it" (p. 73). According to Drucker, successful strategic managers and leaders are those who become change leaders. These individuals identify opportunities and threats to the organization and subsequently establish an environment wherein people can meet these challenges while still growing as individuals.

One of the most important factors for senior managers or leaders is to recognize their ability to critically think their way through a problem. More and more books are being written about the self-organizing abilities of nature and the need to better understand the concept of chaos, Chaos Theory, and complex systems. To the manager and leader, any event that does not comply with their own cause-and-effect database is chaos. Chaos in the past has been an unacceptable condition to managers and leaders. The military have even coined a phrase to capture a chaotic situation in wartime; i.e., the *fog of war*. Although this phrase is being used more frequently beyond military circles, the rationale for its usage is that events occur with so many competing factors that make it difficult to ascertain an appropriate course of action. What is really occurring is that once individuals face situations that are outside their personal database, recognized patterns are lost and chaos becomes operational. We all face this through our childhood and schooling years as well as continuously throughout life. Due to the increasing pace of activities and events today, it is a continuous struggle just to keep up with new emerging patterns that we deal with every day. Chaos may well be the new norm for our daily lives.

According to *Webster's Dictionary* 'chaos' is defined as "A state or place of total confusion or disorder" (1994, p. 248). Of course, this leaves us with the same dilemma we have when people use the word 'leader,' namely, "what are they really saying?" A "state of total confusion" implies that it depends on the knowledge base of the beholder. Another way of saying it is used by James Gleick (1987) when he writes, "Where chaos begins, classical science stops." What is being said in both cases is that due to a limited knowledge base what is being perceived is too complex for the observer and, as people, through research and their experiences, become more knowledgeable, they also become more aware of the underlying order of seemingly random acts.

It is necessary at this point that the text is now moving into the philosophical and theological aspects of the words 'manager' and 'leader.' Specifically, is everything that occurs in the universe the result of pre-determined universal patterns? In Ralph Stacey's book, *Managing the Unknowable* (1992), he provides valid insights as to the frustration in co-existing between the knowable and unknowable worlds. He cautions, as Dee Hock does in his Chaordic Organization and Peter Senge in his *Fifth Discipline* (1990), that today's managers and leaders need to be less concerned with the "illusory goal of a stable equilibrium and allow them to cope with the unknowable future of innovative organizations" (p. 8). Immediately it may seem that this flies in the face of our comment that the POMC model is a universal touchstone process. On the contrary, it reinforces Figure 3.5 (revisited here as Figure 6.1) demonstrating that the structures of the traditional mechanistic organization need to evolve to more free-flowing designs that allow the co-existence between deterministic actions people can take in everyday work life and an unknowable future that needs constant innovation and creativity.

A liberal arts view of the world is needed to broaden one's view. When one hears the words 'Liberal Arts,' the reflex image is a college education. The point is that receiving a liberal arts education in a college is

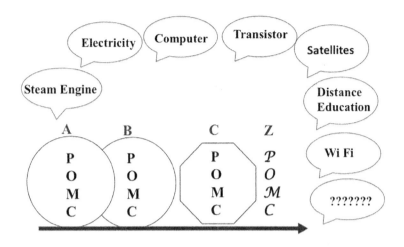

Figure 6.1 Organizational transformation events

not, and should not be, the only path to broaden one's view. Specialization skills are critical for solving clearly defined tasks with a reasonably bounded reality. However, to understand the diversity of activities that occur both internally and externally to organizations in today's environment demands new mental frameworks that Margaret Wheatley, Dee Hock, Peter Senge, and many others have been recommending for years. A common theme for these writers has been to study the patterns of nature that they feel may hold the keys to good management practices. In two classic texts, Charles Handy's *The Hungry Spirit, Beyond Capitalism: A Quest for the Purpose of the Modern World* (1998) and Margaret Wheatley's *Leadership and the New Science* (1999), the linkage to a desire of humans to model their organizational efforts to processes in nature is evident.

The idea of organizations as a living organism has been around for years, however, it was Ludwig von Bertallanfy, a biologist, who is credited with introducing the notion of a "general systems theory" when studying the activities in organizations. When teaching at the U.S. Army War College, Robert introduced his students to the concepts of Wheatley and Handy in order to enhance their insights as to the applicability of these concepts to the military. In addition, having one of the students critique Wheatley's book, Robert showed Wheatley's video explaining her position on using nature as a guide for designing future organizations. The response by senior military and civilian students was initially, "it won't work in the military."

After Robert led the seminar dialogue about the pros and cons on the video and Wheatley's concepts, he focused the dialogue by saying that the then Chief of Staff of the Army, General Gordon R. Sullivan, had read her book and invited her to join a special group of scholars and businesspeople to dialogue on the evolution of organizations, in this case, the military organization. Contrary to the usual caricature of the military where everyone is robotic in their actions, especially even with a four-star endorsement, everyone did not buy in to Wheatley's thesis of tying human organizational development to occurrences in nature.

To provide some background on the U.S. Army War College, it should be noted that its students are educated in critical thinking and complex executive-level problem solving culminating in a Master of Arts degree in Strategic Studies. Additionally, most of the students are in their forties with at least eighteen years of experience of leading and commanding complex military and civilian organizations. As expected, the military and government structure that they grew up in were Industrial Age, mechanistic structures. Through the years, the military was being forced to be more flexible due to evolving technology and the asymmetrical tactics of opposing forces. This was the reality that General Sullivan was attempting to address with a special task force of businesspeople and scholars who had experience in "managing organizational change." Robert is not sure that all his students bought into this new mindset, but it did give them pause for thought as they readied themselves for their new senior positions both nationally and internationally.

Most people will say that this conceptual approach is just another fad by the management community, a sure sign that they have run out of new theories to sell to the world at large – maybe so. But to those of us who have been studying the field of management for a long time, the message always has been there. It has just taken a back seat to those who want a nice, neat approach to the world. With all the events occurring in the world today, it is easier to see that the traditional mechanistic view of the world is unraveling and that a more realistic view is needed to address the turmoil in today's organizations. It is also easier to see that there is a tug of war between generations like ours who were educated and worked in primarily mechanistic organizations and today's generation who see the world in a very fluid, chaotic existence. Additionally, it creates a very real challenge for employees to separate their expectations for their managers and those expectations that they have for their leaders.

Leaders and managers in chaordic organizations

Back in the 1980s, Tom Peters and Nancy Austin in their book *A Passion for Excellence: The Leadership Difference* (1985) wrote about excellence in the corporate world in a relatively stable and predictable environment.

Later Peters wrote in his book *Thriving on Chaos: Handbook for a Management Revolution* (1987) that the stable environment no longer exists. Peters credited this instability to the environment. One might say that Toffler's *Future Shock* (1970) is upon us in full force and the implications for Management theory in an unpredictable, chaotic organizational environment are just beginning to be explored.

Although the implications and pertinent theories will be worked out in years to come, managing change is the challenge for all organizations. Some managers and leaders will resist and think that managing day-to-day activities is just an exercise in attaining an effective and efficient operation. Those who are attuned to the challenges in today's environment will realize that seemingly routine actions are not routine but an unending series of events that form the future of the organization.

Charles Handy (1998) asserts that courageous managers will move boldly when the unlikely happens; they will embrace change and subsequently learn from experiences where the models and rules are not always there to follow. These individuals will overcome resistance to change and unproductive behavior by understanding people and blending individual strengths and teamwork to solve problems and increase productivity and quality. Continuous improvement to management processes will be used by dynamic and prospering organizations. Critical thinking and systems thinking will be used to create and sustain a culture of continuous improvement. The successful manager and leader will deliberately strive to create a positive and dynamic working environment, develop teamwork, apply analytical methods, and use the creativity of all employees in their unit. This environment will be characterized by an energized, collective effort to define, assess, and improve all significant processes, the POMC model, within the organization. Those who fail to do so will find themselves in organizations with rampant suboptimization and competing efforts while trying to get on the same sheet of music.

Managers in the twenty-first century will be continually challenged to review their roles and responsibilities while those who hope to lead will be challenged to find new ways to inspire employees to internally embrace the pace and changes needed for their organization to survive. To do this, individuals must seek to blend the basic theories of management with non-traditional approaches in order to do their jobs better. A primary managerial task will be to instill a corporate vision that the organization lives by in order to provide quality goods and services with limited resources. It will be necessary not only to make decisions for today, but also to anticipate those of tomorrow. To anticipate the needs of tomorrow will require involvement of the entire workforce – not a new message to many managers, or to those who write on the subject. Knowing that workers need to get involved is one thing, getting them decisively involved is another.

Tomorrow's workforce will need to be highly skilled and well educated, and will need to apply knowledge more fully than many have in the past. Because of employee diversity, organizations have the potential to be stronger if managers can successfully blend the different values, knowledge, and backgrounds in the workplace to achieve common goals. For leaders, the task is more daunting. They need to get their employees to believe. If organizations continually up the ante with incentives to get employees to buy in, the competitive edge for organizations will be less responsive and diluted in its creative efforts.

The conundrum, however, is that the way managers diagnose problems and their precision in recognizing the need for change will affect the change process itself. The success of a change program depends largely on the current levels of dissatisfaction, support by top management for the change effort, and the correct diagnosis of the sources of resistance to the change effort. Partnerships in and outside the organization will be essential. The best managers and leaders will promote constant improvement, proactive management, and elimination of barriers. The individuals also will redefine the concept of control as well as how an organization organizes itself.

Organizations will need to continue to focus the energy of their resources in order to survive, but they must do so with different rules, techniques, and procedures than before. This should not be interpreted to mean that all the lessons learned from the past are now discarded, but rather that Toffler's Third Wave society demands different ways of managing and leading. In some cases, drastic changes are needed, in others, subtle changes. In all cases, managers and leaders need to be attuned to the patterns and trends that are continually developing around and within their organization. Then and only then can these managers and leaders have a chance to move their organization toward a viable future.

7   Conclusions

The purpose of this book is to help readers better understand the nuances between being a leader and being a manager. This text should help guide and apprise the reader of the impact that these roles play on decision-making efforts as organizations evolve, especially during transformative times. Although this text is not a substitute for a basic management text, it was necessary to lay out the discipline of management in order to drive a wedge between the terms 'leader' and 'manager.' The hope is that readers will gain a deeper appreciation of management as more robust than it is given credit for. There appears to be a general tendency that when managers or leaders are solving organizational problems, they are quick to discard the lessons that the various theories teach and move directly into problem-solving mode based on their instinct and past experiences.

Some may ask, "What is wrong with that?" The answer is that using one's instincts and past experiences is not wrong, but it is not the total picture. What a deeper understanding of management offers is a resource of accepted theories that will help frame the issues to be resolved. Thus, through this deeper understanding of management, in combination with critical thinking, one can better frame the questions that will address the core issues. In doing so, one may find an answer, or at least a partial solution to the problem at hand.

Management is not a business phenomenon that is relegated to only for-profit-driven organizations. It is an intrinsic process of all organizations that attempt to harness human energy in order to accomplish common goals. As the Information Age forces people within organizations to sort and critically evaluate the myriad of information that is readily becoming available, an orderly process becomes even more necessary. Many management thinkers in the past have provided invaluable insights into who we are at work. The continuing theme appears to be that we are not working to discover the intrinsic order of the universe, but rather that we ourselves are an integral part of the universe. Thus, as we stake out temporary relationships to achieve common goals, critical thinkers, managers, and ultimately leaders need to be mindful that there are indeed temporary relationships fixed by reference points that we ourselves fixed. How long these reference points remain fixed is, and always will be, left to the discretion of managers and leaders and those following them.

Lastly, the world is so enamored with the concept of leaders that the expectations placed on these individuals often fall short and add more stress than necessary when dealing with daily challenges. In conclusion, as probably was the case with Alexander the Great, cutting the Gordian Knot does not fully solve the problem at hand. With this thought in mind, based on the authors' years of interfacing with managers, leaders, and workers, here are some salient points that will help cut through the ambiguity of who is a manager and who is a leader, and more importantly, assist in the alignment of one's expectations:

- Employees need to understand the difference between managers and leaders and adjust their expectations accordingly.
- Managers are not the enemy; they are the organization's duly appointed representatives.
- Everyone is *not* capable of being a manager or a leader. This is not bad but realistic.
- All managers are not leaders; and conversely, all leaders do not make good managers.
- True leaders are chosen by the people (followers), not the organization.
- Good organizational leaders get employees to internally accept the vision and mission of an organization. Bad organizational leaders get people to internally buy into a dysfunctional vision and mission.
- Organizational leaders are best during transformational times, but if none are available, managers still need to ready their organizations for the future while understanding their limitations to get people to internalize the new mission and goals.
- When people do not 'buy in' internally, no one is leading.

We hope our sword was sharp enough to help sever the Gordian Knot and release the realities between being a manager and a leader.

Selected resume of
Dr. Robert M. Murphy

Education

Ph.D. in Social Foundations, State University of New York at Buffalo; MBA in Management, Florida State University; BA in Chemistry, Gannon College

Professor

Professor of Management, Department of Command, Leadership and Management, U.S. Army War College, 10 years

Chair, Management Sciences and Marketing Departments, St. Bonaventure University, 2 years

Assistant to the President for Planning, Institutional Research and Assessment, St. Bonaventure University, 3 years

University-level teaching in Management and Leadership, 22 years

Founder and Administrator: Carlisle Strategic Management Consortium, CEO-level forum on strategic issues, 4 years

Lecturer

International and national lecturer on Managing Organizational Change, Leadership, and Strategic Planning, 16 years

Selected Groups

NASA; U.S. Senate Republican Leadership; Boston Consulting Group; Allied Signal, American Standard; Pennsylvania Department of Transportation; GE; Chrysler; Central Intelligence Agency; Defense Commissary Agency; NW Region, Department of Forestry; Department of the Army, G6; Gannett

Visiting Professor

Yunnan Finance and Economics University, China
Center for Creative Leaders, Poland

Books

Managing Strategic Change, 2000 and 2003, U.S. Army War College, Carlisle Barracks, PA

Liberal Arts Colleges Adapting to Change: Survival of Small Schools, 1996 (Co-author), Garland Publishing

Leading and Managing in the Strategic Arena: A Reference Text (editor), 1996–1997, U.S. Army War College, Carlisle, PA

Case

Case 11, U.S. Army War College: The pursuit to educate future strategic leaders. In Robert Lussier and Christopher Achua, *Leadership* (2004).

Articles

Over 10 articles published and presented at national or international conferences on the topics of Managing Organizational Change, Leadership and Strategic Planning in United States, Germany, Switzerland, Costa Rica, Scotland, Hungary, Czech Republic.

Military Experiences

Retired U.S. Army Officer. Selected assignments included Branch Chief and Staff Officer, U.S. Army HQs Europe, 4 years; Battalion Commander, 2 years; 4th Infantry Division Staff, 4 years; Research assignments, 6 years

Selected resume of
Dr. Kathleen M. Murphy

Education

Ph.D. in Social Science, University of Denver; MBA, St. Bonaventure University; MS in Education, St. Bonaventure University; BS in History/Spanish, Mercyhurst College

University Professor

Penn State University, Hazleton, 6 years; St. Bonaventure University, 10 years; Wilson College, 1 year

Visiting Professor

Yunnan Finance and Economics University, China

Training and Consulting

Creative Leaders Center, Kludzienko, Poland
Commonwealth of Independent States Education Conference, Moscow and St. Petersburg, Russia
Paul Loebe Institute, Berlin, Germany
Political Problems of German Unification United Nations Specialist to Warsaw, Poland
Education Administrators, Western New York; Management Development Center, General Electric, Crotonville, NY
German Political Academy, Tutzing, Germany

Selected Publications

"Biti ali ne biti jrganicen, to je zdaj vprasanje – to be or not to be organic, that is the question." Nase Gospodarstvo, Revjija za Aktualna Gospodarska Vprasanja, Stevilka 3–4, Maribor, Yugoslavia, 1991, pp. 286–289.

"Equity and respect issues related to manufactured home owners in mobile home rental parks." Housing and Society, 1993, Vol. 20.2, 15–23.

"Poland 2000: Beyond the bottom line," 11 July 2000; available from www.sba. muohio.edu/abas/.

"Poland in profile: Where is she now? An assessment of values." *The Journal of Language for International Business (JOLIB)*, 2001, Vol. 12:1, 69–86.

"Under construction: The homeland of Poland." *Organization Development Journal*, Fall 1991, Vol. 9, 66–71.

"We who come to teach are the ones who learn." *Journal of Management Education*, November 1991, Vol. 15, 391–396.

Selected Presentations

Keynote Speaker – Global Competition, Institute of Management Accountants and National Management Association.

Ready, willing and able: Women, an untapped resource. 10th World Organization Development Congress, Berlin, Germany.

Bibliography

Bateman, T. S., & Zeithaml, C. P. (1993). *Management and strategy*. Homewood, IL: Irwin.

Bonvillian, G., & Murphy, R. (1996). *Liberal arts colleges adapting to change: The survival of small schools*. New York: Garland Publishing.

Christensen, C. M. (1997). *The innovator's dilemma: When technologies cause great firms to fail*. Boston: Harvard Business School Press.

Cummings, T. G., & Huse, E. F. (1989). *Organization development and change* (4th ed.). St. Paul, MN: West Publishing.

Deane, P. 1965. *The first industrial revolution*, London: Cambridge University Press.

Drucker, P. F. (1994). *Post-capitalist society*. New York: Harper Business.

Gleick, J. (1987). *Chaos: Making a new science*. New York: Viking Press.

Griffin, R. W. (2013). *Management* (7th ed.). Boston: Houghton Mifflin.

Handy, C. (1995). *The age of paradox*. Boston: Harvard Business School Press.

Handy, C. (1998). *The hungry spirit: Beyond capitalism*. New York: Broadway Books.

Hess, P., & Siciliano, J. (1996). *Management: Responsibility for performance*. Boston, MA: McGraw-Hill.

Hock, D. (1999). *Birth of the chaordic age*. San Francisco: Berrett-Koehler.

Kurzweil, R. (1999). *The age of spiritual machines: When computers exceed human intelligence*. New York: Penguin Books.

Mintzberg, H. (1994). *The rise and fall of strategic planning*. New York: The Free Press.

Mondy, R. W., & Premeaux, S. R. (1994). *Management: Concepts, practices, and skills: A global perspective*. Upper Saddle River, NJ: McGraw-Hill.

Murphy, R. M. (1975, October–November). Management: A business or organizational phenomenon. *Army ROTC Newsletter*, 9(5).

Murphy, R. M. (2000, July 2–5). *Strategic management vs strategic leadership*: *Untying the Gordian Knot*. Paper presented at Academy of Business and Administrative Science conference, Budapest, Hungary.

Pasmore, W. A. (1994). *Creating strategic change*. New York: John Wiley and Sons.

Peter, L. J., & Hull, R. (1969). *The Peter principle*. New York: Bantam Books.

Peters, T. (1987). *Thriving on chaos: Handbook for a management revolution*. New York: Alfred A. Knopf.

Peters, T., & Austin, N. (1985). *A passion for excellence: The leadership difference*. New York: Random House.

Porras, J., & Silvers, R. (1991). Organization development and transformation. *Annual Review of Psychology, 42*, 51–78.

Robbins, S. R., & Coulter, M. (2013). *Management*. Boston, MA: Prentice Hall.

Schermerhorn, J. R., Jr. (1996). *Management*. New York: John Wiley and Sons.

———. (2005). *Management*. New York: John Wiley and Sons.

Senge, P. M. (1990). *The fifth discipline: The art and practice of the learning organization*. New York: Doubleday.

Stacey, R. D. (1992). *Managing the unknowable: Strategic boundaries between chaos and order in organizations*. San Francisco, CA: Jossey-Bass.

Stogdill, R. M. (1974). *Handbook of leadership: A survey of theory and research*. New York: The Free Press.

Toffler, A. (1970). *Future shock*. New York: Bantam.

Toffler, A. (1980). *The third wave*. New York: Bantam.

Vinge, V. (1993, March). *The singularity*. Paper presented at the VISION-21 Symposium by NASA Lewis Research Center and the Ohio Aerospace Institute, Westlake, OH.

Webster's II new riverside university dictionary. (1994). Boston, MA: The Riverside Publishing Company.

Weihrich, H., & Koontz, H. (1993). *Management: A global perspective*. New York: McGraw-Hill.

Wheatley, M. J. (1999). *Leadership and the new science: Discovering order in a chaotic world*. San Francisco, CA: Berrett-Koehler.

Willsen, J. (1996). Critical thinking: Identifying the targets. In R. M. Murphy & M. J. Burkhardt (Eds.), *Leading and managing in the strategic arena: A reference text 1996–1997* (p. 419). Carlisle Barracks, PA: U.S. Army War College.

Wren, D. A. (1972). *The evolution of management thought*. New York: The Ronald Press.

Index

Printed in the United States
by Baker & Taylor Publisher Services